At Issue

Affirmative Action

Other Books in the At Issue Series:

At Issue

Affirmative Action

Paul Connors, Book Editor

GREENHAVEN PRESS
A part of Gale, Cengage Learning

GALE
CENGAGE Learning™

Detroit • New York • San Francisco • New Haven, Conn • Waterville, Maine • London

Christine Nasso, *Publisher*
Elizabeth Des Chenes, *Managing Editor*

For more information, contact:
Greenhaven Press
27500 Drake Rd.
Farmington Hills, MI 48331-3535
Or you can visit our Internet site at gale.cengage.com

For product information and technology assistance, contact us at

Gale Customer Support, 1-800-877-4253
For permission to use material from this text or product, submit all requests online at www.cengage.com/permissions

Further permissions questions can be emailed to permissionrequest@cengage.com

Articles in Greenhaven Press anthologies are often edited for length to meet page requirements. In addition, original titles of these works are changed to clearly present the main thesis and to explicitly indicate the author's opinion. Every effort is made to ensure that Greenhaven Press accurately reflects the original intent of the authors. Every effort has been made to trace the owners of copyrighted material.

Cover photograph © Images.com/Corbis.

LIBRARY OF CONGRESS CATALOGING-IN-PUBLICATION DATA

Affirmative action / Paul G. Connors, book editor.
        p. cm. -- (At issue)
    Includes bibliographical references and index.
    ISBN 978-0-7377-4278-7 (hardcover)
    ISBN 978-0-7377-4277-0 (pbk.)
    1. Affirmative action programs--United States. 2. Discrimination--Government policy-- United States. 3. Minorities--Government policy--United States. I. Connors, Paul G.
    HF5549.5.A34A4212 2009
    331.13'30973--dc22

                                                            2008041617

Printed in the United States of America
    2 3 4 5 6   13 12 11 10 09

ED149

Contents

Introduction

In 1996, Barbara Grutter, a white Michigan woman with a 3.8 grade-point average (GPA) and a favorable Law School Admissions Test (LSAT) score of 161 was rejected by the University of Michigan Law School. The applicant claimed that she was rejected because the law school used race as the main determinant in its admissions process, giving minority applicants an unfair advantage over White and Asian ones with similar credentials. The following year, she sued the university alleging that it had discriminated against her on the basis of race in violation of the equal protection clause of the 14th Amendment to the United States Constitution and Title VII of the Civil Rights Act of 1965. The president of the university, Lee Bollinger, was the named defendant in the lawsuit. Bollinger passionately believed that standardized test scores were not as important as one's race and gender. As a school administrator, Bollinger sought to create and maintain a diverse student body that produced skilled graduates, who, in turn, were able to aggressively compete in a global economy. In 2002, the *Grutter* case was appealed to the United States Supreme Court, which agreed to hear the suit. This was the first time the high court had heard an affirmative action case involving education in a quarter of a century.

In 2003, United States Supreme Court Justice Sandra Day O'Connor wrote the 5-4 majority opinion in *Grutter v. Bollinger* (539 U.S. 306). The decision upheld the law school's "tailored" use of race in admission decisions. Nevertheless, Justice O'Connor opined:

> We take the Law School at its word that it would "like nothing better than to find a race-neutral admissions formula" and will terminate its race-conscious admissions program as soon as practicable.... We expect that 25 years from now,

the use of racial preferences will no longer be necessary to further the interest approved today.

It may surprise O'Connor that within five years of the landmark *Grutter* decision, affirmative action in higher education and state contracting is clearly in trouble. Supporters of racial preferences are troubled not only by the fact that three states have passed ballot initiatives prohibiting racial preferences in admission decisions, but that each of the three states is reliably liberal. The first state to ban racial preferences on college campuses was California. In November 1996, state voters, by an overwhelming margin of 54 percent to 46 percent, passed Proposition 209, which amended the state constitution to prohibit public institutions from considering race, sex, or ethnicity. In Washington state, two years later, voters passed a similar proposal (Initiative 200) by a margin of 58 percent to 42 percent. In 2006, Michigan became the third state in ten years to ban affirmative action at public universities. The Michigan Civil Rights Initiative, despite being opposed by the Michigan Republican Party, the GOP candidates running for governor and the U.S. Senate, and a liberal-left coalition of 180 groups, passed by a margin of 58 percent to 42 percent.

In 2008, Ward Connerly's American Civil Rights Institute, which had spearheaded the state ballot initiatives in California, Washington, and Michigan, targeted four more states. Unlike the earlier liberal states, Connerly is focusing his current efforts on the traditionally conservative states of Arizona, Missouri, Nebraska, and Colorado. On November 4, 2008, dubbed by Connerly as the "Super Tuesday for Equal Rights," state voters had the opportunity to amend their state constitutions to eliminate preferential treatment based on race and gender in public education. Their passage undoubtedly would lead to future ballot initiatives in other states.

The ballot box success of the American Civil Rights Institute certainly has put supporters of affirmative action on the defensive and critics of the practice on the offensive. These sentiments pervade many of the selections in this book. For example, former University of Michigan president Lee Bollinger argues that diversity matters because it offers inherent value to the college experience. Other authors debate Justice O'Connor's prediction that affirmative action will no longer be needed in 25 years; whether racial and gender preferences actually hurt minorities; and the role that objectivity plays in mainstream and ethnic media reporting of affirmative action. With females outnumbering males in incoming college classes, another controversial issue addressed by authors in this book is whether males are, or should be, beneficiaries of gender preferences. Other contributors discuss the GOP's commitment to affirmative action and the impact Barack Obama's presidential candidacy will have on the future of racial preferences in this country. The issues surrounding affirmative action are many and varied and continue to challenge American society.

1

Diversity Is at the Heart of Affirmative Action

Lee Bollinger

Lee Bollinger is president of Columbia University and previously served as president of the University of Michigan.

Unfortunately, too many Americans wishfully think that racial discrimination is a practice of the past. Those who favor a strict merit-based admissions policy are blind to the stark reality that public schools and universities are increasingly unable to carry out their mission to maintain a diverse student body borne of affirmative action. It is an established fact that performance in high school and on standardized tests is far less important to public universities than one's race or gender. A diverse student body is a necessity in today's interconnected world because it produces skilled graduates who can compete in a global society.

During this frantic admissions season, it is easy for our applicants to think that the most important moment in their college career is when they rip open the mail to find out where they got in and where they didn't. But we in higher education understand that the admissions process has less to do with rewarding each student's past performance—although high performance is clearly essential—than it does with building a community of diverse learners who will thrive together and teach one another.

When it comes to creating the kinds of diversity we sorely need in this country, however, disturbing trends and setbacks are making it difficult for many public schools and universities to succeed. The reality is that as much as we may want to believe that racial prejudice is a relic of history, conscience and experience tell us better.

Even now, the [United States] Supreme Court is considering two public-school cases out of Washington and Kentucky that would subvert the resounding principle that *Brown v. Board of Education* established . . . on May 17, 1954, that "separate is inherently unequal." If successful, both cases would ban local districts from developing voluntary desegregation programs that seek to maintain racial balance in our schools and counteract the worst resegregation crisis we have faced since the early days of the civil-rights movement. [The Court, in a 5 to 4 decision, rejected these programs on June 28, 2007.]

Higher education must not lose the practical and political battles to maintain racially, ethnically, and socioeconomically diverse student bodies.

Education Is Segregated

According to the 2000 census, only 14 percent of white students attend multiracial schools, while nearly 40 percent of both black and Latino students attend intensely segregated schools where 90 percent to 100 percent are from minority groups. Further, almost half of all black and Latino students attend schools where three-quarters or more students are poor, compared with only 5 percent of white students; in extremely poor schools, 80 percent of the students are black and Latino.

Beyond elementary and secondary schools, higher education continues to face its own challenges, including statewide bans on affirmative action. Recent news reports have noted how hard some of our leading public universities are working to revise recruitment and admissions policies to comply with those bans without jeopardizing the diversity of the students who attend their campuses. What's important, however, is why those universities are trying so hard to maximize diversity—even though no law requires it, and in several states affirmative action is explicitly forbidden.

I have been deeply involved in two U.S. Supreme Court cases—*Gratz v. Bollinger* and *Grutter v. Bollinger* (2003)—that ultimately upheld the constitutionality of affirmative-action policies at public universities. Let me suggest why, having vindicated the legality of affirmative action, higher education must not lose the practical and political battles to maintain racially, ethnically, and socioeconomically diverse student bodies.

Opponents of affirmative action forget [the] broader purpose in their demand for what they see as a "pure" admissions meritocracy based on how students perform in high school and on standardized tests.

Affirmative Action Is Essential to Students

Universities understand that to remain competitive, their most important obligation is to determine—and then deliver—what future graduates will need to know about their world and how to gain that knowledge. While the last century witnessed a new demand for specialized research, prizing the expert's vertical mastery of a single field, the emerging global reality calls for new specialists who can synthesize a diversity of fields and draw quick connections among them.

The experience of arriving on a campus to live and study with classmates from a diverse range of backgrounds is essential to students' training for this new world, nurturing in them an instinct to reach out instead of clinging to the comforts of what seems natural or familiar.

Affirmative-action programs help achieve that larger goal. And the universities that create and carry them out do so not only because overcoming longstanding obstacles to people of color and women in higher education is the right thing to do, but also because policies that encourage a comprehensive diversity help universities achieve their mission. Specifically, they are indispensable in training future leaders how to lead all of society, and by attracting a diverse cadre of students and faculty, they increase our universities' chances of filling in gaps in our knowledge with research and teaching on a wider—and often uncovered—array of subjects.

Past Education Performance Is Less Important

Opponents of affirmative action forget that broader purpose in their demand for what they see as a "pure" admissions meritocracy based on how students perform in high school and on standardized tests. But it is far less important to reward past performance—and impossible to isolate a candidate's objective talent from the contextual realities shaping that performance—than to make the best judgment about which applicants can contribute to help form the strongest class that will study and live together.

For graduate schools and employment recruiters, that potential is the only "merit" that matters, because in an increasingly global world, it is impossible to compete without already knowing how to imagine, understand, and collaborate with a diverse and fluid set of colleagues, partners, customers, and government leaders.

By abolishing all public affirmative-action programs, voters in California and Michigan (and other states if affirmative-action opponents are successful) have not only toppled a ladder of equal opportunity in higher education that so many of us fought to build and the Supreme Court upheld in 2003. They will almost assuredly make their great public universities less diverse—and have, in fact, done so in California, where the impact has become clear—and therefore less attractive options to potential students and, ultimately, less valuable contributors to our globalized society.

As the president of a private university, I am glad that independent institutions retain the autonomy to support diversity efforts that make our graduates more competitive candidates for employers and graduate schools, as well as better informed citizens in our democracy and the world. But as an alumnus of one public university and a former president of another, I worry about a future in which one of America's great success stories slides backward from the mission of providing generations of young Americans with access to an affordable higher education.

All of this leads to the conclusion that diversity—one of the great strengths of American education—is under siege.

Diversity Is a Great Strength

From the establishment of the land-grant colleges in the 1860s to the GI Bill after World War II to the Higher Education Act of 1965, our public universities have advanced the notion that in educating college students for the world they will inhabit, it is necessary to bring people together from diverse parts of society and to educate them in that context. Far from being optional or merely enriching, it is the very essence of what we mean by a liberal or humanistic education.

It is also vital for establishing a cohesive, truly national society—one in which rising generations learn to overcome the biases they absorb as children while also appreciating the unique talents their colleagues bring to any equation. Only education can get us there.

As [United States Supreme Court] Justice Thurgood Marshall knew so well: "The legal system can open doors and sometimes even knock down walls. But it cannot build bridges. . . . We will only attain freedom if we learn to appreciate what is different and muster the courage to discover what is fundamentally the same." Cutting affirmative action short now only betrays that history of social progress. And, in the process, it threatens the core value of academically renowned public universities at a time when many Americans list rising tuition costs as one of their gravest economic concerns.

American Education Is Under Siege

All of this leads to the conclusion that diversity—one of the great strengths of American education—is under siege today. At the elementary- and secondary-school levels, resegregation is making it exceedingly difficult for minority students to get the resources that inspire rising generations to apply to and then attend college. At the same time, the elimination of affirmative-action programs at our public universities is keeping admissions officials from lifting those same students up to offset the structural inequalities they had to face in getting there.

As we honor the parents, students, lawyers, and nine justices who spoke with one voice in *Brown* on that May day 53 years ago, we would all do well to remember that when it comes to responsible diversity programs—those that help our public schools and our great public universities fulfill their historic roles as avenues of economic and cultural mobility—what is wise is also what is just.

2

Affirmative Action May Hurt More than Help Blacks and Hispanics

John Fund

John Fund writes the weekly "On the Trail" column for the Wall Street Journal *Web site.*

In 2003, United States Supreme Court Justice Sandra Day O'Connor wrote the 5-4 majority decision in Grutter v. Bollinger. *The court upheld the University of Michigan Law School's use of racial preferences to promote diversity. In the opinion, O'Connor thought that in another 25 years the use of affirmative action will no longer be necessary. Five years after this ruling, O'Connor is apparently oblivious of the growing evidence that racial preferences may actually hurt the chances of blacks and Hispanics of graduating from college. If this is correct, then affirmative action has failed miserably and has been an unsound idea from its very inception.*

Sandra Day O'Connor had an enormous impact during her 24 years on the [United States] Supreme Court. In many cases she played the "swing justice" role on the court that Anthony Kennedy does today. On Friday [April 6, 2007] she returned to Washington to revisit one such case, *Grutter v. Bollinger*, the 2003 case in which a 5-4 majority, led by Justice O'Connor, upheld the University of Michigan Law School's use of racial preferences to promote "diversity"—a justification first put forward by the late Justice Lewis Powell in the 1978 *Bakke* case.

Justice O'Connor spoke at a Washington and Lee University symposium honoring Powell, a good friend of hers who retired from the court in 1987. She explained how his reasoning in *Bakke* informed her own opinion in *Grutter*, but she also expanded on some of the cautionary language she had included in her 2003 opinion: "The court expects that 25 years from now the use of racial preferences will no longer be necessary to further the interest approved today."

The whole affirmative action enterprise has been . . . failing to achieve its most basic aim: increasing the number of minority college graduates, doctors, lawyers and other professionals.

In her speech on Friday, she said that preferences should be viewed as "a temporary bandage, rather than a permanent cure." She noted that the public has expressed opposition to preferences at the ballot box. Voters in California, Washington state and most recently Michigan have now banned their use in public universities and contracting. (Florida abolished them without a ballot initiative.) That means the original meaning of the 1964 Civil Rights Act—that racial discrimination of any kind is illegal—has won reaffirmation in three liberal states. Justice O'Connor noted that next year up to nine additional states will be voting on similar proposals—"as is their right and privilege to do so."

Justice O'Connor continued to defend her original position. She lamented statistics that showed that as a result of California's Proposition 209 (passed in 1996) only 2.2% of UCLA freshmen were black, and a fifth of those were on athletic scholarships. (California's overall population is 6.1% black.)

Affirmative Action May Be Flawed Public Policy

She seemed strangely unaware, however, of the growing evidence that racial preferences might have actually decreased the likelihood that blacks and Hispanics will graduate from college. Put differently, if the body of evidence is correct, the whole affirmative action enterprise has been deeply and tragically flawed from the beginning, failing to achieve its most basic aim: increasing the number of minority college graduates, doctors, lawyers and other professionals.

Affirmative action often creates the illusion that black or other minority students cannot excel.

Other panelists at the Powell symposium discussed the work of UCLA law professor Richard Sander, which shows that minority law students in California who attend law schools at which their academic credentials do not match the credentials of other students are less likely to pass the bar exam than they would have been if they had attended less prestigious law schools where their academic credentials would have been closer to the norm. As a result, according to Mr. Sander, there are fewer minority lawyers than there would have been under colorblind admissions. Justice O'Connor did not attend the rest of the symposium and made no reference to the Sander study in her remarks.

Academic Ability Matters

Moreover, Justice O'Connor's comments about UCLA obscured an important and promising real story. While it's true that black and Hispanic enrollment at UCLA and Berkeley went down after Prop 209, these students simply didn't just vanish. The vast majority were admitted on the basis of their academic record to somewhat less highly ranked campuses of the prestigious 10-campus UC [University of California] system, which caters only to the top one-eighth of California's high school graduates. In the immediate wake of Proposition 209, the number of minority students at some of the nonflagship campuses went up, not down.

This "cascading" effect has had real benefits in matching students with the campus where they are most likely to do well. Despite what affirmative action supporters often imply, academic ability matters. Although some students will outperform their entering credentials and some students will underperform theirs, most students will succeed in the range that their high school grades and SAT scores predict. Leapfrogging minority candidates into elite colleges where they often become frustrated and fail hurts them even more than the institutions. It creates the illusion that we are closing racial disparities in education when in fact we are not. While blacks and Hispanics now attend college at nearly the same rate as whites, only about 1 in 6 graduates.

Affirmative action often creates the illusion that black or other minority students cannot excel. At the University of California at San Diego, in the year before race-based preferences were abolished in 1997, only one black student had a freshman-year GPA of 3.5 or better. In other words, there was a single black honor student in a freshman class of 3,268. In contrast, 20% of the white students on campus had a 3.5 or better GPA.

There were lots of black students capable of doing honors work at UCSD. But such students were probably admitted to Harvard, Yale or Berkeley, where often they were not receiving an honor GPA. The end to racial preferences changed that. In 1999, 20% of black freshmen at UCSD boasted a GPA of 3.5 or better after their first year, almost equaling the 22% rate for whites after their first year. Similarly, failure rates for black students declined dramatically at UCSD immediately after the implementation of Proposition 209. Isn't that better for everyone in the long run?

Universities Try to Undermine Ban on Affirmative Action

University admissions officers don't think so. Ever since race-based admissions ended in California, they have tried to do end-runs around the ban and reinstate de facto preferences. For example, UCLA's new "holistic" approach to admissions, which purports to take into account applicants' "whole person," including nonacademic achievements and obstacles they have overcome, was adopted in response to Proposition 209. The results have been dramatic. The number of black students admitted for the 2007–08 academic year has surged by 57%, to 3.4% of the overall student body.

Racial preferences were intended to help disadvantaged minorities, but in reality they have turned into a spoils systems for the privileged.

But the increased numbers come at a cost. As Peter Schmidt reported in the *Chronicle of Higher Education*, the number of students from Asian backgrounds fell to 43.1% from 45.6%. Almost all of the drop came from two groups whose numbers on campus had been rapidly growing: Chinese-Americans and Vietnamese-Americans. "The overall number of minorities seems to have fallen using criteria that downplay academics and substitute factors designed to boost minority numbers," notes one UCLA professor.

Also, in a classic example of the law of unintended consequences, the efforts to factor in the disadvantages students have faced appear to have backfired. Mr. Schmidt notes "there was actually a decline in the number and share of admitted students who are the first in their families to attend college and coming from households that make less than $30,000 annually." Last year, UCLA admitted 24% of such students. This year, under its more "holistic" approach, the share of those with disadvantaged backgrounds who were accepted fell to 17%.

Improving K–12 Education for Minorities Is Key

Racial preferences were intended to help disadvantaged minorities, but in reality they have been turned into a spoils system for the privileged. "Most go to children of powerful politicians, civil-rights activists, and other relatively well-off blacks and Hispanics," says Stuart Taylor of *National Journal.* "This does nothing for the people most in need of help, who lack the minimal qualifications to get into the game."

That's why efforts to improve K–12 education should be emphasized. Justice O'Connor ended her talk by explicitly recognizing that affirmative action, whether successful or not, isn't the real answer to the educational gap preventing minority students from succeeding as well as they might. "We have to make sure we are maximizing their educational potential when they are 8 rather than when they are 18," she said. "We are falling down in that area."

Indeed, many obstacles that have nothing to do with a need for more resources stand in the way of improving the educational performance of minorities. Those include burdensome teacher-certification programs, a failure to involve parents more in the education of their children, rules that hamper school principals, weak-kneed politicians and powerful teacher unions wedded to the status quo.

School choice and other dramatic efforts to improve the quality of K–12 education would do far more to improve the chances of minorities entering and finishing college than any racial set-asides. Indeed, school choice would represent genuine "affirmative action" in favor of millions of disadvantaged kids trapped in failing schools.

3

Mainstream Media Report Unfairly on Affirmative Action

Jacqueline Bacon

Jacqueline Bacon is an independent scholar whose research and writing focus broadly on historical questions about language, empowerment, activism, and social justice.

In the aftermath of a recent United States Supreme Court decision limiting the use of race in public school admissions, many in the media voiced a reactionary view toward diversity and education. In doing so, the conservative media wittingly advanced a longstanding scheme to use the moral authority of the civil rights movement and the historic 1954 high-court decision Brown v. Board of Education *to overturn legal doctrines of racial fairness and inclusion. By championing this divisive strategy, conservatives in the media illogically contend that policies seeking school integration are tantamount to laws mandating discrimination.*

The June 2007 [United States] Supreme Court decision sharply limiting the use of race in public school admissions was viewed with dismay by many educators, civil rights activists and others who support diversity in our nation's public schools. As Ted Shaw, the director of the NAACP Legal Defense and Educational Fund, explained, "In the context of segregated public schools in this country, our experience, almost without exception, is that segregation has always been a prelude to other forms of deprivation, educational and otherwise,

Jacqueline Bacon, "Miseducation," *Extra!*, vol. 20, November/December, 2007, pp. 8–10. Reproduced by permission.

for black [people]." While segregated public schools mean unequal resources and opportunities, education researchers and social scientists have demonstrated that diverse classrooms lead to positive academic outcomes and students better equipped to thrive in a multicultural society.

Media Have Reactionary View of Diversity

For many in the media, however, the occasion was one to celebrate. Their reaction is not surprising, of course; as has been well documented by FAIR and others, numerous media outlets have taken a conservative approach to affirmative action in their reporting and commentary (not to mention in the racial composition of their newsrooms).

Their coverage, though, is problematic not only because it illustrates some journalists' reactionary views about diversity and education, but also because it is misleading, unfair and inaccurate. Many in the media have unquestioningly parroted and endorsed the assumptions and language of the Supreme Court's majority, as well as of the petitioners (the Seattle, Washington and Louisville, Kentucky parents suing the school districts). Even though the majority opinion is deeply flawed and at times disingenuous, and the petitioners' cases are necessarily highly biased, their perspectives and representations have been presented as factual and conclusive.

Pundits and reporters have, in turn, ignored aspects of the dissenting case that would temper or undermine such conclusions, in some cases making false statements that inaccurately bolster the petitioners' case, or relying on stereotypes and glib, questionable presumptions. Perhaps most disturbingly, they have affirmed the attempts of the Court's majority to cast their decision as in the spirit of the landmark 1954 *Brown v. Board of Education* in particular and the civil rights movement in general, a strategy that, as dissenting justice John Paul Stevens put it, constitutes a "cruel irony."

School Integration Is Still Needed

Chief Justice John G. Roberts, Jr., who wrote the majority ruling, added in a concurring opinion, "The way to stop discrimination on the basis of race is to stop discriminating on the basis of race." This near-tautology was offered as a compelling and conclusive assertion in editorials supporting the decision in the *New York Post, Las Vegas Review-Journal, Augusta Chronicle* and Fort Wayne *News-Sentinel,* as well as in columns by Steve Chapman (*Chicago Tribune*) and George Will (*Washington Post*). The *Wall Street Journal* called the declaration a "bedrock principle."

Repeating Roberts' words, these outlets endorsed the ideological strategy Roberts and the right in general follow when discussing affirmative action or plans to achieve integration or diversity. As E. Washington Rhodes explained in the African-American newspaper the *Philadelphia Tribune,* "The chief justice both ignores the continued impact of racial discrimination and the distinction between considering race as a factor to ensure integration rather than to maintain segregation." In other words, Roberts proposed both that there was no ongoing need for proactive plans to combat segregation—no discrimination that couldn't be stopped by simply ignoring race—and that the Seattle and Louisville school districts' plans were equivalent to segregationist policies that showed prejudice toward children of color.

The former assumption is, of course, false; as scholars and policy experts have been reminding us for years the result of residential segregation and white flight is, in many areas, highly segregated schools. Many pundits pronounced, though, that we no longer have the need for programs fostering integration. "If there are any school districts in this country still purposely attempting to segregate students by color so as to provide lesser educational opportunities to non-whites," the *Las Vegas Review-Journal* opined, "it would be interesting to see them named." This statement is simple-minded at best and disingenuous at worst; the integration programs in question were established to combat *de facto*, not *de jure* [in practice, not in principle], segregation.

Media Outlets Offer False Information

Other pundits ignored reality. "We're desegregated now," Tucker Carlson declared (MSNBC). The *Augusta Chronicle* offered a more moderate but also more muddled assertion:

> Where there are still vestiges of state-sanctioned segregation, there are still remedies available through desegregation orders. But as those remnants of an ignoble era have crumbled, so has the foundation of those desegregation orders.

Arguing against the Seattle School District's plan on Fox News' *Sunday Roundtable*, the *Weekly Standard*'s Bill Kristol remarked: "In the Seattle case, incidentally, the schools are totally integrated." This ignored the fact, detailed in the respondents' brief, that Seattle's schools were segregated until the 1960s, when a series of integration plans like the one Kristol opposes were implemented.

The media have at times offered demonstrably false information about the cases at hand—a serious flaw skewing public opinion toward the petitioners' side.

Pundits also echoed the second implication of Roberts' tautological statement—that plans to achieve diversity by fostering inclusion of children of all races are equivalent to segregationist policies that excluded children of color. Tucker Carlson (MSNBC) summarized the ruling as saying "schools can no longer discriminate on the basis of race." When scholar Dr. Ron Daniels argued in favor of policies promoting racial diversity on Fox News' *Hannity & Colmes*, Sean Hannity pronounced, "You support discrimination, that's the difference between you and me."

George Will (*Washington Post*) cast those who supported plans to foster diversity as racists (as he blatantly misrepresented the rationale for inclusion):

> Although progressive people would never stoop to racial stereotyping, they evidently believe that any black or other minority child, however young or from whatever social background, makes a predictable and distinctive—you might say stereotypical—contribution to "diversity."

Erroneous Assertions

The media have at times offered demonstrably false information about the cases at hand—a serious flaw skewing public opinion toward the petitioners' side. As detailed in briefs both from the petitioner in the Seattle case and the Seattle School District, there are no designated neighborhood schools in the district (nor, in fact, were the petitioners seeking such a plan based on residence, as they explicitly state in their brief).

At times media relied on stereotypes and bigoted, false generalizations about students of color to defend the Supreme Court's decision.

Under Seattle's "Open Choice" plan, the district's brief explains, "students submitted their choices [of high school] in order of preference and assignments were made on that basis so long as seats were available in a school." If a school had too many student applications, "tie-breakers" were used to determine admission, with the first being "whether the student had a sibling already assigned to the school," and the second being either proximity to the school or, in the case of schools with "enrollments deviating more than 10 percentage points from the overall district-wide racial composition," the student's race.

However, the *Wall Street Journal* erroneously asserted that students were "reassign[ed] . . . from their neighborhood schools to new ones based on racial composition." Fox News' Brit Hume and the *Portland Press Herald* offered the falsehood that race was the sole factor or tie-breaker by which admission was decided. Fox News and NPR contributor Juan Williams, interviewed on NPR's *Morning Edition*, argued that the justices were not "opposed to integration" but rather "opposed to anything that would have children judged simply on the basis of skin color." (Williams had published an op-ed in the same day's *New York Times* arguing that "*Brown*'s time has passed," and that policies based on race should be eliminated.)

Stereotypes of Minorities Are Often Used

In the case of the Jefferson County Public Schools (Louisville, Kentucky's school district), the Board of Education's plan, as outlined in the respondents' brief, was based on the mandate that public schools have between 15 percent and 50 percent black students. Residential boundaries are taken into account, so that a student has a neighborhood school, although he or she is able to submit applications to other chosen schools. Assignments were made on "the basis of space and the guidelines"; a student may, indeed, be denied admission to the neighborhood school (as was the plaintiff's son), but may be offered admission to another in a designated cluster of schools.

This complex process was reduced and misrepresented; both the *Portland Press Herald* and the *Wall Street Journal* lumped the Jefferson County Public Schools with the Seattle schools and implied that race was the determining factor rather than one of a list of criteria.

At times media relied on stereotypes and bigoted, false generalizations about students of color to defend the Supreme Court's decision. The *Chicago Tribune*'s Steve Chapman trivialized the goals of integration, perpetuated racist views of people of color and blamed minority communities for educational problems, declaring:

The real educational problems faced by minority kids today are not lack of white students to sit by but inadequate choice, lack of order, a shortage of good teachers and families who don't make a priority of learning.

Tampa Tribune editorial writer Joseph H. Brown, himself African-American, also implicitly blamed people of color for any inequities in educational opportunity: "What goes on in students' homes is more important than what happens in the Supreme Court. Maybe now the groups bent on improving education through litigation can turn their attention there." It is clear, of course, whose homes are in question.

Disappointingly—but not surprisingly, given the prevalence of this disingenuous conservative strategy—supporters of the decision tried to claim the mantle of Dr. King as well.

Conservative Strategy Is Disingenuous

Perhaps the most offensive and troubling part of the Supreme Court's decision for many civil rights advocates was Justice Roberts' attempt to cast his opinion as in the spirit of—indeed as both honoring and furthering—the landmark 1954 *Brown* decision. Roberts argued:

> Before *Brown*, schoolchildren were told where they could and could not go to school based on the color of their skin. The school districts in these cases have not carried the heavy burden of demonstrating that we should allow this once again—even for very different reasons.

Roberts' invocation of history is based on the false premises that laws mandating discrimination are equivalent to policies seeking integration, and that assigning children to schools in order to achieve diversity is akin to the forced segregation the *Brown* plaintiffs faced. Many in the media followed suit.

"Far from overturning *Brown*," the *Denver Post* asserted, "Chief Justice John Roberts' majority opinion paid homage to it by concluding that the 'way to stop discrimination on the basis of race is to stop discriminating on the basis of race.'" The *Augusta Chronicle* remarked that "it runs counter to the very spirit of *Brown v. Topeka Board of Education* for schools—absent an affirmative court desegregation order—to send students to certain schools based on race." Syndicated columnist Charles Krauthammer declared on WJLA-TV's Inside Washington that the decision "reaffirmed *Brown*" because "*Brown* said you may not assign a child to a school on the basis of race, and this decision says you may not assign a child to a school on the basis of race."

Some pundits tried literally to equate the plaintiffs in the *Brown* decision with those in the cases at hand. Editorial writer A. Barton Hinkle of the *Richmond Times-Dispatch* remarked that the actions of "officials in Louisville" who "refused to let Crystal Meredith's son Joshua attend a school close to home because of his skin color" seemed "remarkably similar to the treatment meted out to Linda Brown, the Topeka third-grader who had to ride a bus to a black school even though she could have walked to Sumner Elementary, a white school, just a few blocks away."

The Fort Wayne *News-Sentinel* made a similar comparison:

> *Brown v. Board of Education* in 1954 ... started with a suit by a black father upset that his child had to be bused a long way for school instead of going to the one in the neighborhood, just because of race. One of the cases last week involved a white mother upset that her child had to be bused a long way for school instead of going to the one she wanted, all because of race.

Disappointingly—but not surprisingly, given the prevalence of this disingenuous conservative strategy—supporters of the decision tried to claim the mantle of Dr. King as well.

Pennsylvania's *Lancaster New Era* chided the opponents of the majority opinion: "With the hostile reaction the court's ruling has received, one can assume that the left has given up on Martin Luther King Jr.'s dream that Americans 'not be judged by the color of their skin, but by the content of their character.'"

Chief Justice Roberts was correct, however, when he indicated that he was following historical precedent, albeit not the one he claimed. As Northwestern history professor Nancy MacLean explained, conservatives have altered their strategy since the 1960s, when they explicitly opposed the Civil Rights Movement and decisions such as *Brown*:

> They seized the civil rights movement's greatest strength—its moral power—to defeat its goals. They . . . claimed that civil rights measures themselves discriminated. . . . The former segregationists now portrayed themselves as the true advocates of fairness.

This "calculated strategy," MacLean pointed out, is "avidly promote[d]" by the "Federalist Society, with which Chief Justice Roberts has collaborated and to which the Bush administration looks for judicial nominees." The media, as the coverage of the recent decision indicates, both adopt this strategy and help facilitate its continuance by validating the premises on which it is based. With such a powerful ally, it is no wonder conservatives are celebrating.

4

Minority Press Coverage of Affirmative Action Is Not Objective

Terri L. Towner, Rosalee A. Clawson, and Eric N. Waltenburg

Terri L. Towner is a Ph.D. candidate in the Department of Political Science at Purdue University. Rosalee A. Clawson and Eric N. Waltenburg are associate professors in the Department of Political Science at Purdue University.

An investigation into how mainstream and ethnic journalists covered the 2003 University of Michigan affirmative action cases reveals that mainstream, black, and Latino presses covered the court decisions very differently. Whereas mainstream reporters aim to present both sides of the issue in a balanced fashion, ethnic journalists feel an obligation to report from a minority perspective. In doing so, journalists for black and Latino media outlets gave short shrift to the standards of objectivity and fairness. By tailoring the news to fit the views of their audience, ethnic journalists undermine the idea that the Supreme Court is an honest interpreter of the Constitution.

The U.S. Supreme Court regularly articulates policies of profound political and social consequence. Rarely, however, does it take an active role in the broad dissemination of those policies to the public. Indeed, while members of the executive branch or Congress often appear publicly to make the

Terri L. Towner, Rosalee A. Clawson, and Eric N. Waltenburg, "Media Coverage of the University of Michigan Affirmative Action Decisions," *Judicature*, vol. 90, November/December, 2006, pp. 120–126. Copyright © 2006 American Judicature Society. Reproduced by permission.

case for a given policy, the Court simply delivers its opinion. As a result, the Court's policies are vulnerable to the way in which the media disseminate the news to the public—no small matter inasmuch as the media have a significant bearing on public opinion towards the Court's policies.

While objectivity and fairness are valued by the Black and Latino press, those norms are counterbalanced with the need to report from a minority angle.

This article investigates how different media outlets, particularly the mainstream, Black, and Latino presses, cover Supreme Court policies. To this end, we interviewed journalists from the mainstream and specialized presses who covered the 2003 University of Michigan affirmative action cases or the Supreme Court in general. Journalists seek to present information that is newsworthy, appealing to the audience, accurate, and understandable. To achieve this, they are expected to follow universally recognized norms and values of the profession—objectivity and fairness. These norms influence how journalists receive, select, and present information. Thus, we queried journalists on their selection of sources, their audience, norms, and the effect of exogenous forces on their coverage.

Given the two-sided nature of the affirmative action issue, we expected journalists to be "fair" and "objective" in their coverage of the cases and their selection of sources. We also expected that both the mainstream and specialized presses' content is constrained by the structure of their organizations. Nevertheless, we did not have identical expectations for both media outlets. Unlike the mainstream media, the Black and Latino press are also driven by their mission of advocacy. These specialized media act as a corrective to the mainstream presses' incomplete and often erroneous coverage of minority affairs. Thus, while objectivity and fairness are valued by the

Black and Latino press, those norms are counterbalanced with the need to report from a minority angle. Consequently, we expected journalists from the specialized presses to present news differently from their mainstream equivalents.

University of Michigan Affirmative Action Cases

On December 2, 2002, the U.S. Supreme Court agreed to revisit the issue of the use of racial preferences in higher education in the University of Michigan affirmative action cases. By doing so, it placed itself in the middle of an emotionally charged and controversial issue. The Court had not spoken to the use of racial preferences in higher education since its seminal *Bakke* decision in 1978. There, it ruled that the use of racial quotas or "set aside" programs for minority applicants were unconstitutional. Higher education institutions responded by developing admissions procedures that promoted diversity by using race, gender, and other background characteristics as "plus factors" in their admissions decisions, while avoiding the use of racial quotas.

The Court maintained the use of race based affirmative action programs in higher education, while limiting the form of the programs.

These procedures, however, had not settled the issue, and by the close of the twentieth century the post-*Bakke* affirmative action system was under significant stress; cracks were beginning to appear. In 1996, for example, the Fifth Circuit invalidated the University of Texas Law School's affirmative action admissions program altogether, and five years later, with substantial media attention, the Supreme Court denied certiorari [the court declined the request to review the case]. In 1997 and 1998, California and Washington state banned all forms of affirmative action in state institutions with Proposition 209 and Initiative 200, respectively. Finally, Florida approved the "One Florida" initiative in 2000, ending affirmative action in their state institutions.

Clearly, critics of affirmative action were on the offensive, and successfully so. The policy's supporters, however, could take some heart in the fact that each of these breaks in the system was constrained to a specific region or state. That was all to change with *Gratz* and *Grutter*. Because of their appearance in the Supreme Court, they jeopardized affirmative action policy on a national scale.

The University of Michigan affirmative action cases began in 1997 when disgruntled White applicants filed lawsuits alleging that the University's admissions policies used unlawful racial preferences for minority applicants. Specifically, they contested the undergraduate admissions program's use of a points based "selection index" and the law school's use of race and ethnicity as a "plus factor."

Not surprisingly, given the stakes involved, the cases commanded tremendous attention from interest groups and the media. A record number of *amicus* briefs were filed by groups ranging from the Bush administration to Fortune 500 companies to retired U.S. military leaders to civil rights groups. Newspapers across the country carried the Michigan rulings as their lead headline, along with related reports or "sidebars" placed above the fold.

On June 23, 2003, the Court announced its decisions. It upheld the law school admissions process that allows the consideration of race, but also ruled against the point system used in undergraduate admissions. Justice Sandra Day O'Conner, the majority opinion author in the law school case, held that a diverse student body is a "compelling state interest" and Michigan's policy was narrowly tailored to achieve that goal. Writing for the majority in the undergraduate case, Chief Justice William Rehnquist argued that a point system based on race was not narrowly tailored and therefore was unconstitutional. Taken together, the Court ruled that a university may not employ whatever means it desires to obtain a diverse student body, but if race is used in an individualized manner, it could pass constitutional muster. In the end, the Court maintained the use of race based affirmative action programs in higher education, while limiting the form of the programs. . . .

Black and Latino Press Are Less Objective

Though the mainstream, Black, and Latino journalists covered the Michigan cases from different perspectives and used a variety of sources, all journalists acknowledged the importance of objectivity and fairness. Specifically, journalists from the mainstream and specialized media included both pro- and anti-affirmative action positions.

Thus, all advocated serving the public by offering the opportunity to be informed about the affirmative action issue at hand in an unbiased presentation. Jacques Steinberg, an education reporter for the *New York Times*, explained that there was a balance among his articles:

> . . . I'm writing a piece explaining the decision, and it's not a down the middle piece saying, here's the justices who say they're for affirmative action and why, and here's the justices who said that they're against affirmative action and why. That wasn't my job that day, but . . . if you look at the body of my work: I think there's a balancing. The same guy who writes [that there are] all these colleges applauding the fact that they can continue to practice racial preferences is the same guy who wrote . . . a very human look at the people who would like this law changed. So . . . there's a balance. There's also a balance within the paper.

Representing the Latino media, Ketty Rodriguez from *El Nuevo Herald* explained:

> We try in our articles to reflect all positions. For and against the position, and [we quote] people who can comment on

one side versus the other. So we create balanced articles that will be as impartial as possible. We like to present our readers with two sides of the coin. We present the facts or general ideas and then we make a contrast with opinions that differ. . . .

Despite the emphasis on fairness from the specialized media, it is evident that what is considered "fair" is different for the Black and Latino media than for the mainstream media.

In addition to asking journalists if they reported both the pro- and anti-affirmative action sides, we asked if they felt it was appropriate to be an advocate for one side or the other. All responded that their position was not to be an advocate. In fact, most stated that such behavior was completely inappropriate when reporting the news and should be reserved for the editorial pages. Explaining why she was not an advocate, Linda Greenhouse [New York Times] said:

I was simply reflecting what was occurring. . . . What I try to do is reflect the reality that's occurring, and the reality was that the Michigan position seemed to be attractive to a very wide slot of society . . . to me that was news. Whereas on the other side, because there was really no participation in the debates by organizations beyond those whose own mission . . . was just to defeat affirmative action, there wasn't a lot to say on that side. . . . I felt I had to kind of struggle to reflect the other side that wasn't doing a very effective job of reflecting itself.

For the Black press, Dr. [George] Curry explained:

For news, you're obligated to give the arguments from both sides. You're supposed to write the news story, write the cover story, not be an advocate for anything when you are writing a story.

Despite the emphasis on fairness from the specialized media, it is evident that what is considered "fair" is different for the Black and Latino media than for the mainstream media. Fairness for the mainstream media is presenting both sides of the issue in a neutral and balanced manner. The specialized media also present both sides of the issue, but they present the news with a Black and Latino angle. Several Black and Latino journalists explained that, while reporting on this controversial issue, they struggled to balance their desire to give voice to their minority group with the need to be impartial. Often, the journalists' mission to appeal to the unique interests of their audience outweighed the norms of objectivity and fairness. Andrea Acosta explains:

> I think it is important to present both sides of the story. However, obviously when you are talking about a newspaper that services the Latino community it becomes a bit difficult to be totally impartial. What we try—like good Latinos, we have the intention to favor the rights of Latinos. Here we are talking about values that weigh more on the balance because we feel that we are the voice for the Latino community, generally, a community that does not have a voice. Therefore, you could say that our articles sometimes come out a little less balanced. Generally, however, we reincorporate both sides of all topics.

In addition, consistent with their mission, several Black and Latino journalists indicated that they reported information that was not included in the mainstream media. For the Black press, Dr. Curry explained that the mainstream press failed to include a full description of Michigan's undergraduate admissions policies:

> . . . the most underreported things about the Michigan case . . . [were] all other instances where people get points, for whether you live in the upper North peninsulas . . . whether you are a scholarship athlete, or whether the provost decided to give you extra points, and these things are just as

important because they're given the same amount of points if someone is a person of color. If it is a disadvantaged white, a poor white person, they get the same amount of points. . . . If you tell me all that, I'm going to look at things differently. . . . If you only tell me you are giving 20 points to African Americans, then I have a different point of view. . . . So what irks me about the [mainstream] media is that they have been acting like this is an isolated incident by only referring to people of color. . . .

Different Process, Different Missions

Clearly, the missions of both the mainstream and specialized press affect their coverage of the Supreme Court. The ethnic press's emphasis on presenting stories in a manner that is reflective of their readers' interests influences both their selection of sources and the manner in which they present information concerning the Court and its rulings. For sources, they emphasize actors who are ethnically or racially representative of their audience. As a result, different viewpoints or notions of the issue and the Court are likely contained in their accounts. Perhaps more important still, these presses seem to be more mindful of their audience's interests with respect to certain issues. This leads them to present more detailed information concerning the issue before the Court as well as the effects of the Court's rulings for their readers or those like them.

In short, it appears that the specialized press's mission with respect to their audience encourages them to cover the Court more directly as a political actor that renders decisions with real and substantial policy implications. Therefore, the specialized press's Supreme Court coverage does not contribute to the myth of the Court as an apolitical guardian of the Constitution. Consequently, their readers may hold the Court in less high esteem than the readers of the mainstream press.

The mainstream press's mission, for the most part, is to inform the public in a "neutral" or "objective" manner. This press is less mindful of structuring coverage to play to the unique or special interests of its audience. Instead, its emphasis is presenting the "facts of the story," covering both sides of the issue. Obviously, this affects the mainstream press's selection of sources, leading them to draw on "official" sources and to search out, if necessary, sources to square the coverage. Linda Greenhouse illustrated this point rather well when she noted that she had to seek out information from the anti-affirmative action side to ensure that it was adequately represented. "I really had to sort of labor to cover the other [anti-affirmative action] side because I didn't think [it] was presenting itself in a way that was generally all that newsworthy."

As was the case for the specialized media, the mainstream press's mission affects how they cover the Court, which in turn might well affect how their audience perceives the institution. The mainstream press's emphasis on official sources, balance, and objectivity results in stories emphasizing the formalistic and legal nature of the Court's actions and it as an institution. And this in turn likely contributes to their readers possessing rather high levels of diffuse support for the Court. As [political scientists] [James] Gibson, [Greg] Caldeira, and [Vanessa] Baird put it, "to know the courts is to love them, because to know them is to be exposed to a series of legitimizing messages focused on the symbols justice, judicial objectivity, and impartiality." Although likely true in the abstract, our interviews suggest that the effect of this exposure might vary with the source of the exposure. It might well be that the audiences of the different presses have very different attitudes toward the Court because of the way the Court is presented to them. Resolution of that question, however, must await another day.

5

The Demise of Affirmative Action Is Overstated

Scott Jaschik

Scott Jaschik is the editor of Inside Higher Ed, *an online source for news and opinion about higher education.*

Recently, a group of leading educational scholars unanimously thought that United States Supreme Court Justice Sandra Day O'Connor's 25-year deadline on affirmative action would be nearly impossible to reach. Data reveals that black and Latino students have made small strides in closing the education gap with white and Asian students. Part of the problem is that universities are placing greater emphasis on verbal SAT scores, which translates into the enrollment of more white and Asian students. Another key problem is that schools with large minority populations are more likely to have unqualified teachers.

Five years ago, Justice Sandra Day O'Connor saved affirmative action in public college admissions when she crafted the majority decision affirming the consideration of race in admissions by the University of Michigan's law school. While O'Connor found justifications for the (limited) consideration of race and ethnicity, she also spoke of the need for such consideration to stop at some point. "We expect that 25 years from now, the use of racial preferences will no longer be necessary to further the interest approved today," she wrote.

The American Educational Research Association assembled a group of leading scholars Tuesday [March 25, 2008] to con-

Scott Jaschik, "Doomed to Disappoint Justice O'Connor," *Inside Higher Ed*, March 26, 2008. Copyright © 2008 Inside Higher Ed. Reproduced by permission. http://www.insidehighered.com.

sider the state of affirmative action. Officially they were look-ing at the state of the [*Regents of the University of California v.*] *Bakke* decision that first authorized affirmative action. But they kept returning to O'Connor's deadline and her predic-tion that in 25 years (20 years from today), diversity would be possible without affirmative action.

The unanimous opinion: no chance in hell.

Scholars examined a range of demographic and educa-tional data showing how little progress has been made in nar-rowing key gaps in the educational opportunities available to black and Latino students. Given how slowly American educa-tion changes, they said, the idea that the need for affirmative action will disappear in 20 years is almost impossible to imag-ine. A subtext for their discussion was the reality that some states have shown less patience for affirmative action than did Justice O'Connor and have gone ahead and banned affirma-tive action—and more states are expected to follow suit this year [2008].

If [the University of] Michigan really wants diversity, the justices said, it could just lower standards.

Greater Emphasis on Very High SAT Scores

While much of the panel discussion focused on inequality in American society, another group of institutions was also criti-cized for decisions that—without affirmative action—hinder the enrollment of minority students. Top colleges, the re-searchers said, are putting more emphasis on extremely high SAT scores, even though this means that the resulting pool is increasingly white and Asian.

In a paper called "Is 1500 the New 1280?" Catherine L. Horn, of the University of Houston, and John T. Yun, of the University of California at Santa Barbara, looked at the verbal SAT score averages of students at the 30 top colleges and universities (as determined by *U.S. News & World Report*). At all but four of these institutions, at least 30 percent of the freshman class had scored 700 or greater on the verbal SAT, and at half of these colleges, more than 50 percent of freshmen have such scores. In 1989, only one of the 30 colleges reported that more than 30 percent of the freshman class had a score of at least 700 on the verbal SAT.

The shift is "extreme," Horn said, "suggesting a real shift in admissions toward very high-scoring individuals."

Raising the issue in this way is sensitive for supporters of affirmative action, even if they are skeptics of standardized testing. As Horn noted, two of the Supreme Court justices most critical of affirmative action, Clarence Thomas and Antonin Scalia, wrote a dissent in the Michigan law case in which they pointed out that the law school could easily have a diverse class without affirmative action. They said that a law school like Michigan's could set admissions policies that were relatively open or relatively elitist, and that the former would result in more diversity than the latter. If Michigan really wants diversity, the justices said, it could just lower standards.

Relatively few black and Latino students 20 years from now will end up in elite colleges without some kind of affirmative action.

"No one would argue that a university could set up a lower general admission standard and then impose heightened requirements only on black applicants," the justices wrote. "Similarly, a university may not maintain a high admission standard and grant exemptions to favored races. The Law School, of its own choosing, and for its own purposes, maintains an exclusionary admissions system that it knows produces racially disproportionate results. Racial discrimination is not a permissible solution to the self-inflicted wounds of this elitist admissions policy."

Horn stressed that in questioning the elite colleges' devotion to the highest possible SAT scores, she was not endorsing the Thomas-Scalia view. They are implying, she said, a strict dichotomy between academic rigor and diversity—a dichotomy she called "a false one."

When the elite colleges were admitting students with 600 verbal SAT scores, they were still plenty competitive, she said, and the increase wasn't necessitated by some terrible academic failings of those students or a national rise in scores. Rather she viewed it as part of a sense that higher numbers are always better (since *U.S. News* says so). If colleges stepped back a bit, she said, they would find they could attract very talented (and more diverse) students by focusing on admitting students who are very strong, but not necessarily part of the most elite (and less diverse) group out there.

"What we're talking about is a reconceptualization of merit," she said.

Minorities Receive Inferior High School Education

If colleges are at fault for SAT obsessions, the researchers said, there are plenty of other trends for which the culprit is the failure of American society to tackle educational and economic inequity. The audience heard a range of statistics— most of them "depressing," as one discussant said—that suggest that relatively few black and Latino students 20 years from now will end up in elite colleges without some kind of affirmative action.

For instance, in another paper, Yun cited findings that in California, high schools with large minority populations are 6.75 times more likely than other high schools to have unqualified teachers. By numerous measures, he said, minority students are more likely to attend schools with fewer offerings and to end up with a worse education. For O'Connor's vision to work in 20 years, minority and non-minority students would need to be "virtually indistinguishable" on a range of academic qualities, and the gaps in educational opportunity are too wide today for that to be viable, he said. He called it "very unlikely" that the high school student population 20 years from now would reflect O'Connor's wishes.

Donald E. Heller of Pennsylvania then outlined a series of gaps in high school graduation rates and college enrollment and graduation rates. At every stage along the way, he noted, schools and colleges lose black and Latino students. For example, 84 percent of white students who enroll in 9th grade are enrolled in 12th grade three falls later, while the figures are 61 percent for black students and 66 for Latino students. Those minority students are then less likely to enroll in college and to graduate from college.

Heller's paper focused on his attempts to identify states that have more success than others at closing the white-minority gaps, and he found that the states that do the best job at this are generally states without many minority students period.

The odds of achieving O'Connor's goals in 20 years? "Slim," Heller said.

Minority Enrollment in College Could Get Worse

Gary Orfield of the University of California at Los Angeles agreed. "These problems are not going to be solved" in 20 years, he said. Part of the problem, Orfield said, is that too many people assume that there has been steady progress on educational equity. In fact, he said that while some figures for individual students have improved, there have in fact been two distinct periods since the civil rights movement. In the 1960s and much of the 1970s, the government was creating new programs to promote equity, adding substantially to the budgets of schools and colleges, and demanding evidence that states were educating their minority students.

Much of that stopped in the Reagan administration, he said, and has never really been replaced. Lacking some sort of sustained movement, he said, "nothing suggests we will meet Justice O'Connor's prediction. I think these trends suggest it will get worse."

Orfield suggested that there is a next generation of research topics that education scholars should take on. Among his suggested topics:

- Detailed analysis of the state of educational opportunity in the formerly segregated states of the South. Given the large black populations of these states, much more work needs to be done on the state of educational opportunity and the impact of the withdrawal of federal supervision, Orfield said.

- The impact of students attending largely segregated high schools on their college-going decisions and experiences.

- The social consequences of having large communities where educational opportunity has largely vanished. Orfield said that there is much data on how this hurts individuals, but not nearly enough on communities.

- Latino students and the reasons for their relatively low enrollment and graduation rates in higher education.

Orfield challenged those in the audience to do work that would show what he termed the realities of education today, not the "wishful thinking" of the O'Connor opinion.

6

Sports Is No Place for Affirmative Action

Ari Kaufman

Ari Kaufman is a military historian for the Indiana War Memorials Commission and an associate fellow at the Sagamore Institute for Policy Research.

In 2002, the Black Coaches Association was part of a class-action discrimination lawsuit against the National Football League for not interviewing at least one minority candidate for potential head coaching positions. When the league buckled under public pressure, affirmative action had made it to collegiate and professional sports. More recently, college basketball was criticized for not allowing more black schools into the hugely popular NCAA tournament. Fortunately, the NCAA, unlike the NFL, did not listen to the racial demagogues and maintained the current format.

When the late Johnnie Cochran and other lawyers, with the aid of the "Black Coaches Association" [BCA], passed legislation in 2002 that all National Football League teams must interview at least one "minority" candidate for potential head coaching jobs, the NFL timidly acquiesced, and Affirmative Action had officially arrived in collegiate and pro sports.

In its most blunt terms, Cochran's gang's class-action discrimination lawsuit forced the rules to now decree that re-

Ari Kaufman, "Affirmative Action in Sports," *Front Page Magazine*, March 21, 2006. Copyright © 2006 FrontPageMagazine.com. Reproduced by permission. http://www.frontpagemag.com.

gardless of experience or achievement, a quota of one African American (or other "minority") was to be given a chance at being hired for a football coaching job. Why was this rule necessary? Its advocates said it was, because at the time only three of the 106 Division One college football coaches were black, and only four of 30 NFL coaches were of "minority persuasion." And yes, since the BCA was the impetus behind the move, and since there are few, if any, Latino, Asian, Indian, Jewish, Arab, or Armenian coaches in college or the NFL, then we must assume, as always, that "minority" equals black.

As far back as 1999, radical campuses like City College of San Francisco were already balkanizing racial matters and demanding action and apologies.

Baseless Claims

Four years ago, the National Football League fined the Detroit Lions for not following the new league hiring policies of interviewing at least one minority. The whole process reeks of condescension and most objective observers have noted that, by and large, these required interviews have been a waste of time and money. Naturally though, no one objected to the new rules, likely for fear of being blackballed.

College football has also seen baseless claims of racism. Early in 2005, Notre Dame quickly became the culprit of racial intentions, when they fired Tyrone Willingham, an African American, despite Willingham's lack of success at the demanding football school. The new coach, Charlie Weis, quickly turned the team back into a national power in one season, while Willingham, hired in Seattle by the University of Washington, sputtered to a 2–9 record in 2005.

In the past three years, the number of black coaches in the NFL has jumped from three to seven, while only new hires Lovie Smith (Chicago) and Marvin Lewis (Cincinnati) have seen immediate success. Yet, when a sports writer, talk show host, or ordinary fan questions why more and more teams ([in 2006], the Oakland Raiders re-hired Art Shell, the first black coach in history, who [hadn't] coached in 15 years) are hiring under-qualified black coaches, s/he is quickly deemed a "racist."

These factions began accusing the NCAA of "conference profiling," trying to essentially "rip off" black schools from the publicity and financial gains of the NCAA Tournament.

Yet there are still complaints about the "paucity" [lack] of black coaches in sports. And while some feel the need to play percentage games, thankfully, others like renowned ESPN's Kansas City–based sportswriter, Jason Whitlock, an African-American, have suggestions, and also have put matters into perspective. He described Cochran's efforts as "misguided, outdated and totally ignore the fact that black people, just like every other ethnic group in this country, control their own destiny."

As far back as 1999, radical campuses like City College of San Francisco were already balkanizing [dividing] racial matters and demanding action and apologies.

Accusations of Racial Profiling in College Basketball

The racial demagogues [leaders] have targeted college *basketball*, as well. Most recently, and most noteworthy, when the NCAA basketball tournament brackets were announced, many black coaches, administrators, and media members said schools from predominantly black conferences were playing a disproportionate amount of the NCAA's Opening Round. This was allegedly the case last Tuesday night [March 14, 2006] in Dayton, when Hampton (black school) took on Monmouth (a mostly white school). These factions began accusing the NCAA of "conference profiling," trying to essentially "rip off" black schools from the publicity and financial gains of the NCAA Tournament.

The furor is unsubstantiated. A cursory visit to the history of the "play-in game" shows that no more than half of the schools in such a position could be classified as "black colleges." And, more importantly, a look at their records shows why these schools were the last ones invited into the postseason tournament; that's why they keep standings throughout each season.

This past week, just prior to Tuesday's game, Mike Tirico, an African-American who works for ABC/ESPN, accurately explained that the clamoring was nonsense. Citing first the records of the teams, and also the way the match-ups are determined, he stated it was all in the numbers. Tirico also noted that the teams in the Opening Round Game enjoy all the benefits and luxuries of tournament life, even if for only that one game. If you watch the game, played in hoops crazy Dayton, on national TV, this is extremely evident. The name was even changed from "play-in game," so as to augment the appeal of the game, which seems to elicit more intensity than most first round matchups on Thursday and Friday.

However, for pointing out the truth and not placating the Jackson/Sharpton Lobby's "cause," the esteemed Mr. Tirico will surely be called an "Uncle Tom." And anyone like me and 90% of the country who agrees with him will be called a "racist." The *true* racial-dividers regularly make silly, racist, spurious claims like these.

Opening Round Game Success

Lastly, the general consensus on the game has been positive. Wikipedia.org notes:

Although analysts' initial reactions to the concept were skeptical, the first game, played on March 13, 2001, was a success, and few complaints have been heard since. One reason for these positive comments is the fact that the game is played on a Tuesday night, during which no other games are played (the first round of the tournament starts the following Thursday). Thus, the play-in game assumes a greater prominence than most first-round games, both to the viewing public and to scouts.

ESPN college basketball guru Andy Katz found potential in the game from its inception in 2001, stating, "There were 6,800 fans in the arena, the majority non-partisan, and they didn't seem to mind that these weren't nationally recognizable names. The crowd was into it, and the game actually had more pulse than a 16-vs-1 game at noon Thursday."

Now more than five years later, Katz could certainly not have conceived of a racial objection when he opined, "There was merit to this first opening-round game. It can be better, but it wasn't bad. Two teams feel like they've accomplished something, even if one is going home before most people fill out their brackets. We were wrong. This wasn't a bad idea."

No, it wasn't then, and it still isn't. Much less a racist one. The professional balkanizers will stop at nothing to justify their existence in post-racist America.

7

Affirmative Action for Men Is Politically Incorrect

Melana Zyla Vickers

Melana Zyla Vickers is a columnist for the TCS Daily, a Web site that explores issues related to technology, commerce, and society.

According to projections by the United States Department of Education, by 2010 women will outnumber males in college by a ratio of 60-40. Also, since 2000, white males are the only demographic group whose high-school dropout rate has risen. Although these trends are not new, the enrollment gap is now widening. In many cases, males are not only failing to keep pace with the graduation rates of females, but are losing ground. Some studies suggest that the shortage of men in college is due to the lack of academic focus on the cognitive areas in which boys excel. The shortage of men in higher education is compounded by university bureaucrats who largely ignore or deny the problem. School administrators are not paying enough attention to the academic needs of males because male preferencing is politically incorrect.

Here's a thought that's unlikely to occur to twelfth-grade girls as their college acceptances begin to trickle in: After they get to campus in the fall, one in four of them will be mathematically unable to find a male peer to go out with.

At colleges across the country, 58 women will enroll as freshmen for every 42 men. And as the class of 2010 proceeds toward graduation, the male numbers will dwindle. Because more men than women drop out, the ratio after four years will be 60-40, according to projections by the [United States] Department of Education.

The problem isn't new—women bachelor's degree-earners first outstripped men in 1982. But the gap, which remained modest for some time, is widening. More and more girls are graduating from high school and following through on their college ambitions, while boys are failing to keep pace and, by some measures, losing ground.

Why the blind devotion to gender-blindness? Because affirmative action for men is politically incorrect.

Underperformance in education is no longer a problem confined to black males, Hispanic males, or even poor whites. In 2004, the nation's middle-income, white undergraduate population was 57 percent female. Even among white undergraduates with family incomes of $70,000 and higher, the balance tipped in 2000 to 52 percent female. And white boys are the only demographic group whose high school dropout rate has risen since 2000. Maine, a predominantly white state, is at 60-40 in college enrollment and is quickly reaching beyond it. There are now more female master's degree-earners than male, and in 10 years there will be more new female Ph.D.s, according to government projections. American colleges from Brown to Berkeley face a man shortage, and there's no end in sight.

Male Gender Gap Is Largely Ignored by Colleges

Yet few alarm bells are ringing. In the early 1970s, when the college demographics were roughly reversed at 43 percent female and 57 percent male, federal education laws were reformed with the enactment in 1972 of Title IX, a provision that requires numerical parity for women in various areas of federally funded schooling. Feminist groups pushed the Equal Rights Amendment through the House and Senate. Universities opened women's studies departments. And the United Nations declared 1975 the International Year of the Woman. The problem was structural, feminists never tired of repeating: A system built by men, for men, was blocking women's way.

Today's shortage of men, by contrast, is largely ignored, denied, or covered up. Talk to university administrators, and few will admit that the imbalance is a problem, let alone that they're addressing it. Consider the view of Stephen Farmer, director of undergraduate admissions at the University of North Carolina–Chapel Hill, where this year's enrollment is only 41.6 percent male. "We really have made no attempt to balance the class. We are gender blind in applications, very scrupulously so."

Why the blind devotion to gender-blindness? Because affirmative action for men is politically incorrect. And at universities receiving federal funding like UNC, it's also illegal. "My understanding of Title IX is that an admissions process that advantages men would be very difficult to defend," Farmer says.

The recent history at the University of Georgia, with its male enrollment of 42 percent, explains the situation further. In 2001, a federal appeals court struck down the university's use of gender and race criteria to try to boost its black, male numbers in undergraduate admissions. Three white women sued the school after being rejected, arguing they'd have gotten into the University of Georgia if they had been black men. The appeals court agreed with a lower court's finding that the admissions process in place at the time violated Title VI (race equity) and Title IX (gender equity) by "intentionally discriminating against them based on race and gender."

It didn't even take a court ruling to cause Brandeis University, which is 46 percent male, to abandon its lame effort to attract more men. A few years ago it offered free baseball caps to the first 500 male undergraduate applicants. Brandeis's new dean of admissions, Gil Villanueva, says "things were looking pretty low on the male end and so people said let's give it a shot and see what happens." Evidently not much—the promotion was never repeated. Says Villanueva, "We have no special recruitment plan for males. We are very much gender blind." He says the administrators won't worry about the gender balance unless "all of a sudden our applicant pool is 75 percent female."

Boston University, 40.8 percent male at the undergraduate level, shows even less official concern. The imbalance is a national trend that begins with fewer men graduating from high school and applying to college, says spokesman Colin Riley. "We can't do something about the pool if they're not applying."

BU's position wasn't always so passive. In the mid-'90s, then-president John Silber sought to take a few small steps to address the shortfall of males. He told staff that BU's publicity materials ought to be gender-neutral, and that an ROTC [Reserve Officers' Training Corps] publicity photo showing a woman ought to show a man, because ROTC at the university was predominantly male. Asked this month about Silber's minor intervention, university spokesman Riley tried to downplay it, saying "most places would be impressed" to have a woman in the ROTC photo. He added that the gender ratio is not "discerned as a problem. We certainly don't view it as such." Interesting, then, that BU doesn't publicize the sex breakdown of its student body on its website.

Richard Nesbitt, admissions director at Williams College, which is just 52 percent female, sees things differently. "If we got to 60-40, that would set off some alarm bells because we would like to have a 50-50 split," he says, adding balance is desirable "in terms of the social atmosphere and so forth."

Nesbitt says Williams's past as an all-men's college, plus strong math and science departments and athletics programs, helps keep the male numbers higher than the average. A few other formerly all-male schools, such as Princeton, actually have male majorities. But while the situation isn't yet alarming for such schools as Williams, Nesbitt calls it "alarming in terms of what's happening in our society."

The gender imbalance in the overall college makes departments so segregated that campus life just ain't what it used to be.

The Federal Government and the Press Ignore the Problem

The Department of Education doesn't appear to agree. The home of Title IX enforcement continues to be so preoccupied with advancing women that a recent 50-page study called *Gender Differences in Participation and Completion of Undergraduate Education* focuses not on the shortfall of men that's evident in practically every data point, but on tiny subpopulations of women who still have "risk characteristics," such as those entering university after age 29. And the department still spends money on studies such as *Trends in Educational Equity of Girls and Women: 2004*, while ignoring the eye-popping trends for boys and men.

The neglect has extended to the press as well, though there are a few signs that the blackout may be ending. The *Chronicle of Higher Education*, the bible of college and university news, has hardly touched the issue. *EdWeek*, while it has done better, still devotes less ink to the current gender gap than it does to women. And a recent piece in the *Washington Post* is an encouraging sign. As for state governments, inquiries around the country have turned up only a single public body studying the problem, a commission in Maine that is due to publish a study of boys' underperformance in education in January [2006]. It's true that President [George W.] Bush mentioned boys' troubles in the 2005 State of the Union, but his aim was to "keep young people out of gangs, and show young men an ideal of manhood that respects women and rejects violence." Only a few business groups have looked at young men's academic performance, as have a handful of private researchers and authors.

Yet the trends are grave. Women outstrip men in education despite [the fact] that there are 15 million men and 14.2 million women aged 18–24 in the country. Kentucky colleges enroll at least 67 first-year women for every 50 men. Delaware has 74 first-year women for every 50 men.

Gender Gap Within Colleges

The gender gap is even more palpable within the colleges themselves, because women and men gravitate to different majors. While a split in preferences has always been the case, the gender imbalance in the overall college makes departments so segregated that campus life just ain't what it used to be. In North Carolina's public and private universities, a typical psychology class has four women for every man. In education, the ratio is five to one. The English and foreign language departments are heavily female as well.

The consequences go far beyond a lousy social life and the longer-term reality that many women won't find educated male peers to marry. There are also academic consequences, and economic ones.

Only a few fields, such as business and the social sciences, show men and women signing up at comparable rates. Math, computers, engineering, and the physical sciences continue to be male-dominated (in North Carolina, for example, engineering is 79 percent male), and the total number of graduates in these economically essential fields is often stagnant or declining. Thus, between 1992 and 2002, when the number of bachelor's degree-earners in California's public university system grew by 11 percent, the number of engineering bachelor's degrees shrank by 8 percent. California's private universities fared better, but the gap is still striking: bachelor's degrees grew by 41 percent overall, while bachelor's degrees in engineering grew only 27 percent.

It seems the education system is favoring quantity over quantitative skills. The result? American companies and research organizations that need to employ graduates in quantitative fields have to turn to foreigners. Already, an astounding 40 percent of all the master's degrees awarded by American institutions in science, engineering, and information technology go to foreign students, as do 45 percent of all Ph.D.s in those fields, according to a study of the gender gap in education by the Business Roundtable in Washington, D.C.

The answer that education experts keep recycling is that American girls need to be encouraged to go into quantitative fields. After all, if there's one thing Harvard president Larry Summers taught the nation, it's that questioning women's aptitude for science is an absolute no-no. But surely some reflection is needed on whether science, mathematics, and engineering wouldn't be more attractive to American boys if more of them were encouraged to discover, at an early age, whether they have strengths in those fields and were warmly encouraged to pursue them in their schooling.

We're certainly not seeing any such encouragement these days. While much of the gender imbalance in higher education results from girls' advancing through high school and into university in greater proportions than boys, there are a few categories of boys who are stuck or losing ground. The high school dropout rate for white boys hovers around 7 percent, at a time when girls—black, white, and Hispanic—are making annual progress in cutting their dropout numbers, as are black and Hispanic boys. (To be sure, the Hispanic boys' high school dropout rate remains astonishingly high, and contributes to the overall college imbalance: 26.7 percent in 2003, a rate not seen since the early 1970s among black boys and girls.)

It is boys' lack of skill in . . . noncognitive areas that is the principal cause of the gap.

Young men also drop out of college more readily than young women do. And even in affluent, educated, white suburbs, fewer twelfth-grade boys make plans to attend college than girls do, according to a study by the Boston Private Industry Council. Unfortunately, a student who defers college enrollment increases his odds of never attending. All of this makes the pool of applicants to college predominantly female, and the pool of enrollees more female as well.

Boys Lack Skills in Noncognitive Areas

What is going on? Schools are not paying enough attention to the education of males. There's too little focus on the cognitive areas in which boys do well. Boys have more disciplinary problems, up to 10 percent are medicated for Attention Deficit Disorder, and they thrive less in a school environment that prizes what Brian A. Jacob of Harvard's Kennedy School of Government calls "noncognitive skills." These include the ability to pay attention in class, to work with others, to organize and keep track of homework, and to seek help from others. Where boys and girls score comparably on cognitive skills, boys get worse grades in the touchy-feely stuff. Perhaps not coincidentally, boys reportedly enjoy school less than girls do, and are less likely to perceive that their teachers support them, according to studies of Hispanic dropouts.

Harvard's Jacob is one of the few scholars to have studied the gender gap in higher education. His statistical analysis suggests it is boys' lack of skill in these noncognitive areas that is the principal cause of the gap. Other factors, which include young men choosing to go into the military or winding up in prison, account for only about one-sixth of the spread, according to his calculations.

Even now, almost two decades after the failure of the effort to ratify the Equal Rights Amendment, the culture is still in thrall to feminist orthodoxy.

Plain old economics is at work as well. Consider that among Hispanic boys, the wage gap between high school dropouts and high school graduates is much smaller than for whites and blacks. Hispanic boys may figure that high college tuition and four more years of touchy-feely classroom work is less appealing than a job and an immediate income. The economic draw of the workplace holds great sway over male college dropouts as well. A "need to work" accounted for fully 28 percent of male dropouts' reasons for leaving college, but only 18 percent of women dropouts' reasons, according to a Department of Education study. The men were also more likely than women to report academic problems and dissatisfaction with classes as their reasons for leaving.

The Future Is Not Bright

Whatever the precise combination of causes, the imbalance on today's campuses can only be harmful in its social and economic effects. In a rational world, the Bush administration would take a serious look at whether continued enforcement of Title IX is keeping men away from college. At a minimum, the federal Department of Education would follow the example of the state of Maine and mine its statistics for detailed information about boys. Only then would researchers be equipped to address the problem.

Even now, almost two decades after the failure of the effort to ratify the Equal Rights Amendment, the culture is still in thrall to feminist orthodoxy. The Bush administration declined to do battle against Title IX three years ago, essentially preserving the status quo when college sports teams sued for reforms. Meanwhile, the myopic bureaucrats at the Department of Education are unlikely to take their heads out of the sand unless forced to: As if prompted by the imminent release of Maine's report on how to help boys catch up, the National Center for Education Statistics led its website on December 1 [2005] with a colorful chart displaying the sex breakdown at a single high school—one in Bangor, where it just happens that boys outnumber girls.

8

College Men Are Benefiting from Affirmative Action

Sarah Karnasiewicz

Sarah Karnasiewicz is a deputy editor for the online magazine Salon.

Unlike 35 years ago when the gender ratio on American campuses overwhelmingly favored men, today women are more apt to go to and graduate from college. Recently, there have been numerous articles on the growing academic gender gap and whether it is time to adopt affirmative action for males. This debate, however, is not a recent development. Colleges and universities have been implementing informal affirmative action policies to assist young men for many years. Unlike affirmative action programs for minorities and women, male admission preferencing has been driven underground.

Child psychologist Michael Thompson has devoted his professional life to advocating for America's boys. As the bestselling author of "Raising Cain," he's logged thousands of hours as an educational speaker and makes frequent appearances on national television as an authority on troubled young men. But Thompson is also the father of a 20-year-old daughter. And when asked if, given their much-maligned status in schools these days, boys ought to be given a leg up in college admissions, his answer is blunt: "I'd be horrified if some lunkhead boy got accepted to a school instead of my very talented and prepared daughter," he says, "just because he happened to be a guy."

But that may be just what is happening. Amid national panic over a growing academic gender gap, educators have begun to ask, might it be time to adopt affirmative action for boys?

The statistics are revealing: Fewer men apply to colleges every year and those who do disproportionately occupy the lowest quarter of the applicant pool. Thirty-five years ago, in the early days of widespread coeducation, the gender ratio on campuses averaged 43-57, female to male. Now, uniformly, the old ratios have been inverted. Across races and classes—and to some extent, around the Western world—women are more likely to apply to college and, once enrolled, more likely to stick around through graduation.

I know [affirmative action for boys] is being practiced, especially on liberal arts campuses where the gap is biggest . . . because I've had administrators tell me so.

Even in a vacuum, discussions of gender-based affirmative action would be deeply political. But the possibility of a full-fledged battle appears especially likely these days, as we find ourselves in the middle of what's popularly known as the "war on boys." If you watch the news or read the papers, you know the soldiers: Last year, [First Lady] Laura Bush launched a federal initiative focused on boys who have been neglected by their schools and communities; [writers] Christina Hoff Sommers, George Gilder and Michael Gurian have swarmed the talk show circuit and editorial pages, bemoaning the lack of male role models in American schools and accusing educators of alienating boys by prizing passive, "feminized" behavior such as sitting quietly, reading independently, and focusing on sedentary rather than dynamic projects. (Though Thompson, for the record, says "education has actually become more dynamic and teaching gotten better for boys"—and, I quote, "We used to have to hit them to keep them still.") *New York Times* Op-Ed writer John Tierney made waves in January [2006] with an essay warning that educational success will come back to haunt women as a dearth of educated, eligible husbands turns them into miserable spinsters—and in a rebuttal, *Nation* columnist Katha Pollitt asked why, years ago when she was in school and men made up the majority, no one was worrying about whether they'd find wives. Finally, a few weeks ago [in 2006], *Newsweek* joined the fray with an eight-page cover story by Peg Tyre, breathlessly captioned "The Boy Crisis," and laden with oversize color photos of doleful white boys, seemingly adrift in a sea of competent, well-adjusted girls.

Males Already Benefit from Affirmative Action

With all this coverage, you'd be excused for thinking the debate is a recent development. But the truth is that affirmative action for men, like the gender gap itself, is simply not news. Back in 1999, a young woman filed a federal civil rights lawsuit against the University of Georgia in Athens, after it was revealed that the school had attempted to balance gender on campus by awarding preference to male applicants, much the way it might build racial diversity by assigning extra admissions "points" to minority students. At the time, the school, in its defense, told the *Christian Science Monitor* that it was trying to reverse male flight from campus (at the time the ratio was 45-55) before it "became something bad." Unfortunately for the university, the district court judge assigned to the case wasn't convinced, ruling instead that "the desire to 'help out' men who are not earning baccalaureate degrees in the same numbers as women . . . [was] far from persuasive."

Talk to admissions insiders today, though, and they'll tell you that the University of Georgia case did not so much end affirmative action for men as drive it underground. "My belief is that there are already many informal affirmative action policies," says Thompson. "It is entirely possible that a better qualified girl has not gotten into a school because admissions officers were trying to create a more even ratio." Tom Mortenson, senior policy analyst at the Pell Institute for Opportunity in Higher Education and creator of the *Postsecondary Education Opportunity Newsletter*, who in the mid-'90s was one of the first scholars to draw attention to the gender gap, agrees. "I know [affirmative action for boys] is being practiced, especially on liberal arts campuses where the gap is biggest," he explains, "because I've had administrators tell me so."

Last fall, their interest piqued by the flurry of news stories describing the growing chasm between boys and girls in higher education, Sandy Baum and Eban Goodstein, economics professors at Skidmore College and Lewis and Clark College, respectively, embarked on a close study of admissions data from 13 liberal arts schools, hunting for an unacknowledged preference for men in the admissions process. "I'd just read so many stories about the declining number of men applying to colleges," says Baum, "that it seemed inevitable that the disparity would or already had launched a campaign of affirmative action."

Baum and Goodstein's findings, while not conclusive, did carry weighty implications for the future of college admissions. At the time of their research, explains Baum, the incoming class at every school they studied was still composed of more than 50 percent girls, which made sweeping pronouncements about the prevalence of affirmative action difficult to support. And their profiles of male and female applicants were based primarily on statistical data—a standardized test score or GPA—thereby preventing them from taking into account many of the murky intangibles, like extracurricular activities, recommendations and personal essays, on which many admissions officers rely.

Still, in the case of schools where the gender imbalance was most acute—at colleges that were once single-sex, for instance—and where women consistently accounted for more than 60 percent of applicants, Baum and Goodstein *did* find compelling evidence that male students had a statistically greater probability of being accepted than female students of comparable qualifications. Their conclusion? "There seems to be a kind of affirmative action tipping point that occurs when an application pool becomes too heavily weighted toward women. But the interesting thing is that that point is by no means the 50-50 mark—it's likely closer to 40-60," explains Baum. "So while we did not find widespread gender preferencing, given the trends on campuses, with more and more schools approaching that tipping point, we could certainly see a big change."

And it's not just former women's colleges facing a 40-60 divide anymore. A quick survey of colleges and universities around the nation found that Kalamazoo College in Michigan comes in at 45-55, the University of New Mexico at 43-57, New York University at 40-60, and Howard University at 34-66 (low-income, minority men and women are most affected by the educational gender gap). Michael Barron, director of admissions at the University of Iowa, has watched his school's 44-56 ratio hold steady throughout his nearly two-decade tenure at the university. "We just have consistently had more women than men, and I know there's a lot of schools—like the University of North Carolina, Chapel Hill, for example— that have been even closer to 40-60 for quite some time," he says. As a state-supported institution that, according to Barron, "has a stewardship responsibility to accept students regardless of issues of gender or race," Iowa maintains that it has no intention of "either consciously or subconsciously" differentiating between men and women in the admissions process. But, Barron admits, "I wouldn't want it said that we are unconcerned. We are watchful and mindful and will be looking to see what happens . . . and whether there is a role for colleges and universities to play as part of the solution."

Karen Parker, director of admissions at Hampshire College in Amherst, Mass., reports that for the past three years her entering classes have had an average ratio of 41-59, and that men only account for 38 percent of applicants. "I don't believe that the school needs to be exactly 50-50, but from a cultural standpoint, I do think it's important that we have men engaged," she says. "Hampshire doesn't practice affirmative action right now—but I certainly can't say we won't in the future. It's a really perplexing problem and just not a good sign of things to come."

There is no doubt that schools are trying to market themselves to boys now, just the way they did to women 30 years ago.

Schools Recognize Gender Imbalance

But schools that have not gone so far as to accept male students over more qualified women are still finding ways to shift their admissions agenda toward young men. "There are things schools can and do do," says Christina Hoff Sommers, resident scholar at the American Enterprise Institute for Public Policy Research and author of "Who Stole Feminism?" and "The War Against Boys." "Strengthening their engineering departments, getting a hockey team. Some schools are changing admission documents to appeal to male minds—and I know we're supposed to pretend there's no difference [between male and female minds], but anyone in advertising will tell you there is."

And for sure, many colleges are banking on these differences. "At our national conference each year we invariably have a speaker devoted specifically to recruiting boys," explains David Hawkins, the director of public policy at the National Association of College Admission Counseling. "Now most four-year colleges work with their own internal marketing department or contract out to an independent agency that tailors their marketing to young men—and they are very, very aggressive."

Since teenage boys are often crazy about technology, a number of universities, including Case Western Reserve, Seton Hill and MIT (which, admittedly, at 57-43, doesn't seem to have a problem attracting men), have launched admission-oriented blogs designed to offer an intimate, uncensored look at college life. Other schools take a more subliminal approach, by packing their catalogs with pictures of smiling, confident young men and playing up dark, "masculine" color schemes in mailings.

"There is no doubt that schools are trying to market themselves to boys now, just the way they did to women 30 years ago," says Joseph Tweed, president-elect of the New York State Association of College Counselors and director of college counseling at the Trinity-Pawling School, a private all-boys school in upstate New York. "Everyone is asking, 'How do we do this? Do we change the structure of classes? Do we send out glossier materials?' But I think what worries educators the most is that boys don't seem as focused on the process as girls. [Boys] seem to feel they'll be OK, whereas with girls there's still a sense that if they don't do well, don't go to college, there'll be a consequence that will be negative."

Men Don't Need to Go to College

Tweed's point raises a controversial question that most crusaders in the "war on boys" would rather dismiss. Despite their flagging performance in elementary and high school, men have hardly abdicated their power to women. While women may have held the majority in higher education for more than a decade, men still earn more than women, still hold the vast number of tenure-track university positions. Women possess executive positions at less than 2 percent of Fortune 500 companies. Could it be that men aren't going to college because they don't *have* to?

According to Laura Perna, assistant professor of educational policy and leadership at the University of Maryland, the gender gap is all about economics. Last fall, Perna published a paper in the *Review of Higher Education* in which she determined that young women might be more motivated to pursue higher education because, consciously or unconsciously, they sense that there are real economic advantages at stake. Her examination of a Department of Education sample of more than 9,000 high school students, interviewed over a period of eight years, revealed that women with bachelor's degrees earn 24 percent more than women without, while young men with bachelor's degrees experience no significant economic gains. For practical proof of her hypothesis, one need only consider that most well-paid, skilled, blue-collar professions continue to be dominated by men—while minimum-wage jobs in hospitality and service remain the province of women.

Tom Mortenson, of *Opportunity*, remains skeptical. "I've heard that story, but think of it this way—men have had a 3,000-year head start, while everything women have accomplished has largely been in the last 30 years," he says. "So yes, if you're a big, strong guy, there are jobs out there. But the fields that are growing fastest are in healthcare, education, leisure and travel, and the services—all areas that women are better at than we are. So if guys want access to that world, they'd better get an education that qualifies them. Because they won't be big and strong forever." In the future Mortenson imagines, America's changing economy leaves generations of unprepared, aimless, undereducated and emasculated men wasting away, taking the health and happiness of their wives and families with them. But as with Tierney and some of the other boy crusaders, some of Mortenson's greatest fears aren't focused on the perils facing men who lose course in school, but on the freedoms of women who don't. "On the one hand, you want to embrace the success of women," he tells me. "Yet, as more and more women substitute careers for having babies, I've come to see that we're looking at a population crisis. The most educated women have the fewest children—this is not rocket science, it's just the way things work. We need women to have 2.1 children [in order to maintain the U.S. population], but the recent Census Bureau reports show that American women with bachelor's degrees average only 1.7. You can do the math—if we continue this way the white population is headed for extinction."

It's reasonable to assume that creative forms of admissions preferencing will continue to stir debate.

Having worked for decades to increase educational opportunities across class, race and gender lines, Mortenson knows his talk about women's responsibility to preserve the species will get him in trouble—indeed, it already has. He says his daughter, age 29 and childless (but equipped with a master's degree), won't speak to him on the subject. But even his fatherly concern ("I want my daughter to have it all, but I worry that in old age she'll be lonely") can't disguise some of the insidious implications underneath those concerns: that educated white women might single-handedly be responsible for the decline of Western civilization.

No Decline in Number of Men Graduating from College

In the fall 2005 issue of *Ms.* magazine, Phyllis Rosser wrote that rather than being "celebrated for [our] landmark achievements, [women] have engendered fear," and offers up this fact, conspicuously absent from most media coverage of the gender gap: "There has been no decline in bachelor's degrees awarded to men," she writes. "The numbers awarded to women have simply increased." Put simply, in the words of Jacqueline King, director of the Center of Policy Analysis at the American Council of Education, who is quoted in Rosser's piece, "The [real news] story is not one of male failure, or even lack of opportunity—but rather one of increased academic success among females and minorities."

The boy crusaders believe that the seeds of academic failure are planted in primary school, which raises the question: Why are we waiting until college to redress the problem? "I've read many reports that male middle-school students are lagging behind their female counterparts," says Michael Barron. "So it seems to me that that's where we need to look. Because the fact is, all we have available to us, once people begin applying to college, is a product of what they've done before. Our reaction has to come sooner."

Until that happens, however, and should current enrollment trends continue, it's reasonable to assume that creative forms of admissions preferencing will continue to stir debate. As our phone conversation ends, Michael Thompson's voice turns grave. "I want to make very clear that I do not subscribe to this notion of a 'war' on boys," he says. "I think we have been living in a very exciting time when we have taken the shackles off of girls in education. I loved what feminism did for girls—we got inside them and understood them. My personal mission just happens to be to get people to think about boys with the same depth."

9

Cultural Affirmative Action Is Alive and Well

Selwyn Duke

Selwyn Duke is a frequent contributor to the online publication American Thinker.

A majority of Americans practice cultural affirmative action, which occurs when people make an extra effort to help minorities based upon the latter's identification with a "victim group." Although these people mean well, their actions are dishonest for the practice denies the reality that in some instances a person's race is a benefit. For example, race was truly an advantage for golfer Michelle Wie and President Barack Obama. In many ways, cultural affirmative action is worse than traditional government-sanctioned affirmative action because at least the latter is easily recognizable.

In a way, I prefer the old, overt affirmative action. While it was government-sanctioned discrimination, at least it was, in some measure, more honest than our cultural affirmative action. There is such a thing. It's when people in the market and media privilege others—sometimes unconsciously—based upon the latter's identification with a "victim group."

Probably a majority of Americans in some degree or other practice cultural affirmative action. They have the best of intentions, many feeling an obligation to right history's wrongs. And they point to continuing disparities disadvantaging blacks as a group. So they make an extra effort to be sensitive and maybe once in awhile the ones with power even let their thumb rest on the scale when it comes to redressing past grievances.

Cultural affirmative action manifests in all arenas, not just politics.

This phenomenon is what [1984 vice presidential candidate] Geraldine Ferraro referred to recently when she addressed Barack Obama's meteoric political rise and said, "If Obama was a white man, he would not be in this position." Pundits have condemned her for this unfashionable utterance, but it's no insight. It's a truth hiding in plain sight.

Cultural Affirmative Action Is Real

What do you think Bill Clinton was referring to when he said that he wanted his cabinet to "look like America," meritocracy [based on skill] or quota orthodoxy [based on diversity]? Yet Clinton isn't alone; he merely gave voice to common practice. Would Joycelyn Elders (the poster girl for AA [affirmative action]) have been [United States] Surgeon General if she weren't a black woman? Would Ruth Bader Ginsberg and Sandra Day O'Connor have ascended to the Supreme Court and Janet Reno been Attorney General if they weren't female? And, as Ferraro noted herself, she would never have been the 1984 vice-presidential candidate but for her fairer-sex status.

Cultural affirmative action manifests itself in all arenas, not just politics. A perfect example is Michelle Wie, the female golfer who set her sights on tackling the men's tour. Based mainly on braggadocio and a fawning media bent on portraying her as an Amazon golfer who would teach the boys a lesson or two, she was granted entry into numerous PGA tournaments, even though untold numbers of male golfers were more deserving. Of course, some will point out that she is quite gifted. Others will say that the market spoke.

> *The idea that [Barack] Obama's race is an asset is so true that even the scoffers sometimes unwittingly affirm it.*

That is my point.

Sure, Wie is no duffer, just as the other folks I mentioned have their talents; Ginsberg, O'Connor and Reno know how to negotiate the law, Ferraro understands politics and Elders can provide comic relief. Yet ability wasn't the factor most relevant to their rise. As for the market, that is precisely the entity that effects cultural affirmative action. People glommed onto Wie at least partially because they believe that breaking down sex barriers is healthy and that her success would have represented another step forward in female/male equality. Cognizant of this "market," politicians, media outlets, and others know that if their hires and appointees don't "look like America," America—or at least its squeakiest wheels—will look at them with suspicion.

As for Obama, I personally know of a white man in Illinois who supports him because he "... always wanted to see one [a black man or a woman] in the White House."

Cultural Affirmative Action Is Dishonest

This may or may not be a wise or just practice for voters. But as with most other aspects of cultural affirmative action, we are not allowed to notice it. It is taboo. The idea that Obama's race is an asset is so true that even the scoffers sometimes unwittingly affirm it. Writing at MercuryNews.com, Ruben Navarrette characterized Ferraro's comments as "bitter, envious and foolish" and wrote,

> "As Republican strategist and CNN contributor Leslie Sanchez noted, it takes chutzpah for someone who herself

benefited from the politics of gender to accuse someone else of benefiting from the politics of race."

Note that Sanchez did not say that Ferraro was *wrong*; she simply implied it was hypocritical for her to level such an accusation.

Yet denial of the obvious isn't uncommon. I heard both Bill O'Reilly and Dick Morris (whose predictions usually don't match the reliability of a weather forecast) both dismiss Ferraro's assertion. How can politics wonks be so blind? Or is it that they will not see?

It depends on the individual. Some people are so imbued with leftist orthodoxy that they interpret everything through the black=oppressed/white=privileged prism and divide their world into victims and victimizers. By their lights, the idea that a social phenomenon could benefit the former is too preposterous to consider.

They may be doing no favor to blacks with this attitude. Writing in the *Financial Times*, Christopher Caldwell notes a just-published book:

> A very interesting book published this week shows why. In *Racial Paranoia* the University of Pennsylvania anthropologist John L. Jackson Jr. suggests that extravagant theories of white racism—from the widespread AIDS rumour to Louis Farrakhan's allegation that the US actually blew up the levees to cause the deadly New Orleans floods during Hurricane Katrina—have their roots in the decorous language that mostly white leaders have invented for talking about race.

> The US has not managed to eliminate racism, Mr. Jackson thinks, but it has succeeded in eliminating racist talk. Remarks the slightest bit "insensitive" draw draconian punishment. White people, because they feel thoroughly oppressed by this regime, assume that it must be some kind of "gift" to minorities, especially blacks.

> It is not. It is more like a torment. It renders the power structure more opaque to blacks than it has ever been, leav-

ing what Mr. Jackson calls a "scary disconnect between the specifics of what gets said and the hazy possibilities of what kinds of things are truly meant." If the historic enemies of your people suddenly began talking about you in what can fairly be called a secret code, how inclined would you be to trust in their protestations of generosity?

Uncomfortable Truth

But then, to paraphrase George Orwell, in every age there is a big, uncomfortable truth that no one dares mention. In many cases, this simply means lying, paying homage to the dogma of the day so as to avoid becoming anathema. Yet in other cases the lie takes a more subtle form.

Discerning an unfashionable truth presents one with a dilemma. He either must profess it, which can mean career destruction and ostracism—being loathed by others—or he can refuse to do so, which, if he is sincere of heart, can mean he will loathe himself. In other words, if he withholds it, he may feel like a phony; worse still, if asked about it, he may feel compelled to *lie*. The latter especially makes it hard to like yourself.

So many choose a different route: They lie to *themselves*. It isn't difficult; all that is necessary is to deny the matter its day in your mind's court. If you simply refuse to examine all the relevant facts—if you avoid searching for the truth—there is little danger of finding it. It's that famous human ability known as rationalization.

Perhaps you thought affirmative action was in its death throes, with all the state referenda and court rulings against it. We have the cultural variety, and it will be with us a while longer. Maybe long enough for people to be able to talk about it.

10

Barack Obama's Candidacy Shows that Affirmative Action Is Still Needed

Ari Melber

Ari Melber is a correspondent for The Nation.

In 2008, the nation, for the first time, elected a black president of the United States. Earlier, Colin Powell and Condoleezza Rice were selected to be the country's secretaries of state. Many pundits interpret these racial milestones as proof positive that affirmative action is no longer needed. However, talented black leaders like Barack Obama rose to national prominence because they benefited from affirmative action policies. It is imperative that universities, particularly law schools, continue to ensure minorities access to higher education. Despite these high profile exceptions there are too few top-tier black political leaders.

In America's long struggle for racial equality, 2007 was a paradoxical year. Just as our political system seriously contemplated a black President for the very first time, the [United States] Supreme Court declared the end of racial integration policy, halting voluntary local remedies to desegregate public schools under *Brown vs. Board of Education*. Presented with the rise of Barack Obama and the fall of *Brown*, most people have focused on the good news.

Many Americans were captivated by the self-proclaimed "audacity" of Obama's January [2007] announcement that he

Ari Melber, "Obama, Race, and the Presidency," *The Nation*, January 3, 2008. Copyright © 2008 by The Nation Magazine/The Nation Company, Inc. Reproduced by permission.

was running for President. Obama made it clear he was not running to send a message or to register voters but literally to get elected. His campaign initially worked because the political elites accepted this unprecedented proposition. Reporters took Obama's candidacy seriously from its inception, and the donors did, too. Obama has already secured more than a footnote in history, shattering records for individual contributors to his campaign. Win or lose, he is arguably the first black American to be treated by the political and media establishment as a fully viable presidential contender. It is an achievement that cannot be claimed by any other racial minorities. (Jesse Jackson's campaigns did not attain such standing with the political establishment, despite their significance for many voters.) We should not gloss over this development. It is a meaningful step towards addressing a resilient, uncomfortable American fact: our national power structure has always been, and stubbornly remains, overwhelmingly white, from all forty-three Presidents across history to ninety-five of the one hundred senators serving today.

Hostility towards affirmative action runs so deep, in fact, it is a staple of attacks against black political candidates.

Public Opposes Affirmative Action

That segregated power structure was reinforced by the Supreme Court's sharply divided June decision to ban integration programs in public schools. Most educational policies that consider a student's race for the purposes of integration are now illegal. Like the original *Brown* opinion, this year's decision is not neatly confined to K–12 schools, either. *Brown* consecrated a new national ambition for racial equality in the public sphere, delegitimizing both explicit and implicit racism in government, and laying a foundation for remedial measures to equalize many other facets of our society. Many critics contend that this case, *Parents Involved In Community Schools v.*

Seattle School District No. 1, augurs a disturbing slide backwards. It bans integration programs, sharply restricts race-based government remedies and sets the stage for future bans on other remedial programs, such as affirmative action, as Justice Stephen Breyer warned.

But will the public really stand for this sweeping attack on *Brown's* legacy?

Yes. In most of the country, public opposition towards measures to remedy America's history of racial discrimination, from academic recruitment to professional affirmative action, has actually outpaced the conservative court. Even putting aside the South, generally liberal electorates—including California, Washington and Michigan—have passed state referenda completely banning affirmative action. Hostility towards affirmative action runs so deep, in fact, it is a staple of attacks against black political candidates. Senator Jesse Helms perfected coded campaign racism in 1990, with an infamous attack ad darkly juxtaposing his black opponent's face with the text "For RACIAL QUOTAS." Which brings us back to Barack Obama.

Some commentators have latched onto Obama's success as proof for the flawed claim that the United States has completely achieved equal opportunity for all, obviating remedial programs like affirmative action. "Obama embodies and preaches the true and vital message that in today's America, the opportunities available to black people are *unlimited if* they work hard, play by the rules, and get a good education," writes Stuart Taylor Jr., a columnist for *The National Journal* (emphasis added). Taylor presents one man's unusual political arc as a universal lesson for all "black children": "Obama's soaring success should tell black children everywhere that they, too, can succeed, and they do not need handouts or reparations." Obama's success is definitely inspirational, but is that because it is an average example or a remarkable exception?

Obama Is Not An Affirmative Action Candidate

As a politician, Obama is an accomplished black man who knows that some voters still see him, before all else, as "the black candidate." It seems as if commentators either fixate on how his blackness makes his candidacy historic—as I just did—or debate whether he is "black enough." Obama dutifully protests these lines of inquiry, assuring audiences that his qualifications, vision and personal experiences transcend race. This is not only true, it is a political necessity. Obama knows that he is unlikely to win as the "black candidate," let alone the "affirmative-action candidate."

Few other campaigns in recent memory have pressed meritocratic [skill-based] credentials as forcefully as Obama's aides. Today's candidates tend to downplay their Ivy League educations in favor of more humble qualifications. Yet it is rare to hear Obama's history discussed without a reference to Harvard, or his prestigious stint as editor-in-chief of its *Law Review*. Even when his campaign is not emphasizing it, reporters highlight Obama's education far more than any other candidate's. Take, for example, articles from the major newspapers about the leading Democratic candidates in the first ten months of this year's [2007] campaign. Obama's Harvard Law credentials turn up a whopping 178 times—six times the thirty Yale references for Hillary Clinton. John Edwards's law school was only mentioned once, in an article about how he met his wife.

This emphasis is vital to Obama's candidacy. He earned his past success and current prominence, in this narrative, as evidenced by his academic achievement and intelligence. The story line aims to banish the racist thought, lurking beneath our public discourse, that perhaps this candidate succeeded only because of his race. Sometimes it seeps out anyway. During a January [2007] appearance on Fox News, columnist John McWhorter offered the baseless claim that "the reason that

[Obama is] considered such a big deal is simply because he's black." McWhorter implausibly continued, "If you took away the color of his skin, nobody right now would be paying him any attention."

Such baseless attacks obviously predate Barack Obama. Even the most extraordinarily successful minorities are either attacked for their achievements, or the meaning of their educational and professional advancement is contested. Like other talented, smart and successful black Americans who have broken barriers (including [former Secretary of State] Colin Powell and [current Secretary of State] Condoleezza Rice), Obama excelled in an institution that used affirmative action to propel qualified minority applicants. Having proven their mettle as leaders, it is clear each of these figures would excel without affirmative action. And no one knows how their careers would have developed in a society without remedial measures for discrimination. Yet their paths show how the United States has benefited from applying affirmative action in public institutions.

Rice has emphasized how affirmative action gave her an opportunity to prove herself in academia. "I myself am the beneficiary of a Stanford strategy that took affirmative action seriously," she told a Stanford faculty meeting in 1997, and her rise through academia and government embodies the policy's four original rationales: minority students can overcome adversity, excel academically, share their perspectives to enrich a diverse student body and benefit from the requisite training for leadership positions in society, eventually helping to redress the effects of hundreds of years of discrimination. In other words, by pursuing the values of adversity, diversity and redress on campus, universities can both improve their educational offering and advance equality across American society. Americans are decidedly mixed on "affirmative action"—both as a literal program and as a vessel for complex emotions about race—but few would openly challenge those values. Yet those values have not driven the debate for a long time.

Minorities Need Access to Power and Education

In 1978, the Supreme Court struck down a University of California affirmative action program and rejected most of the program's traditional rationales. Adversity and redress were out. Instead, Justice Lewis Powell carved out narrow legal authority for programs advancing "diversity," based on the university's special First Amendment right to foster diverse and open educational environments. "The atmosphere of speculation, experiment and creation—so essential to the quality of higher education—is widely believed to be promoted by a diverse student body," he declared.

The opinion would have profound "discourse shaping effects," as Yale Law School Professor Jack Balkin has written, because advocates of affirmative action could no longer defend the program's legality by citing illegal rationales. So an administrator might support affirmative action because people who overcome adversity have qualities that tests do not reflect, or because redressing a history of racist exclusion enhances the institution's legitimacy, but those arguments were suddenly out of bounds. The courts specifically required "diversity" to justify affirmative action.

Depicting affirmative action solely as a diversity measure not only departs from the program's original purposes. It is also a tough sell. For example, when a 2003 Gallup poll simply asked white Americans whether they "favor" affirmative action, 44 percent said yes and 49 percent said no. When the same poll offered a more detailed choice between college affirmative action "to help promote diversity" or admissions operating "solely on the basis of merit," however, white support for affirmative action plummeted 20 points. Blacks and Hispanics, who favored affirmative action by higher margins, also backed off in this question, with support dropping 21 and 27 points, respectively. Severed from other rationales and pitted against merit, it turns out that even for sympathetic Americans, "diversity" is a drag on affirmative action's validity. Apparently the public imagination prefers bootstrap narratives to the gauzy diversity of Benetton ads.

In order to cultivate a set of leaders with legitimacy in the eyes of the citizenry, it is necessary that the path to leadership be visibly open to talented and qualified individuals of every race and ethnicity.

It took another twenty-five years for the Supreme Court to move beyond its cramped conception of diversity as the only acceptable rationale for affirmative action. In 2003, the Court broadened the legal foundation for the policy. In a five-to-four decision, the Court cited an influential amicus brief from one of the most aggressive proponents of affirmative action, the US military. A group of former Defense Secretaries and Chairmen of the Joint Chiefs explained that beyond the largely intrinsic benefit of diversity, the very legitimacy and efficacy of the military was advanced when its leadership looked like the rest of the enlisted soldiers. The brief declared that a "highly qualified, racially diverse officer corps educated and trained to command our nation's racially diverse enlisted ranks is essential." The Supreme Court largely adopted that view, through Justice O'Connor's majority opinion, touting the importance of diverse national leadership for the entire country:

[U]niversities, and in particular, law schools, represent the training ground for a large number of our Nation's leaders. Individuals with law degrees occupy roughly half the state governorships, more than half the seats in the United States Senate, and more than a third of the seats in the United States House of Representatives. The pattern is even more striking when it comes to highly selective law schools. A handful of these schools accounts for 25 of the 100 United States Senators, 74 United States Courts of Appeals judges, and nearly 200 of the more than 600 United States District Court judges. In order to cultivate a set of leaders with legitimacy in the eyes of the citizenry, it is necessary that the path to leadership be visibly open to talented and qualified individuals of every race and ethnicity. All members of our heterogeneous society must have confidence in the openness and integrity of the educational institutions that provide this training.

Thus the Court finally conceded that programs ensuring minorities have access to education and power are important for public legitimacy and redressing past discrimination. After all, the lack of "diversity" among today's leaders is a product of historical discrimination. (The discrimination ranges from the obvious, like voter suppression, to the obscure, like college legacy preferences that function as grandfather clauses for mostly white alumni.) The Court still talked about diversity, since it was the only accepted rationale within the relevant precedent, but it became a vessel for other, underlying grounds that had been pushed off the stage.

Republicans Refuse to Admit Use of Affirmative Action

This "diversity in national leadership" approach also received an important boost from an unlikely benefactor: George W. Bush.

Liberals and conservatives rarely discuss it, but Bush applied affirmative action to select his cabinet, elevating more racial minorities to senior positions than any administration in American history. That includes, of course, two secretaries of state (officially the highest-ranking cabinet post), a national security adviser, an attorney general and the secretaries of commerce, labor, transportation and housing and urban development. Contrarians might claim that all those barriers were broken by accident, in a colorblind process that just happened to make history.

Yet the record reveals Bush's deliberate use of affirmative action. Bush went out of his way to find black candidates in a Republican Party that grooms virtually no black politicians for the national stage. (There are no black Republican members of Congress, and only seven percent of black Americans self-identify as Republicans, according to a 2004 study by the Pew Research Center.) Finding qualified black leaders required a rare detour from the GOP's overwhelmingly white, partisan networks. It is no surprise that the President tapped the two American institutions at the forefront of affirmative action, the military and the academy, to select former general Powell and former provost Rice.

Ultimately, one part of the high public regard for bright, talented successful black leaders . . . stems from public awareness that our country is still struggling to overcome racial barriers.

Why doesn't Bush get more credit for using affirmative action to build the most diverse cabinet in American history?

He refused to preach what he practiced.

In a conservative twist on "politically correct" culture, Republicans often banish the language of affirmative action even when they practice it. While Bush consciously recruited minorities into some of the most important positions in the United States, he would not admit it. Instead, he spoke out against affirmative action, claiming to advocate only "race-neutral" programs, and thrust his Solicitor General into the odd position of arguing against the President's own policies in the 2003 affirmative action case before the Supreme Court.

We Still Need Affirmative Action

The Administration lost, of course, in the decision written by Justice O'Connor. Now she has been replaced by Samuel Alito, who is widely expected to be the fifth vote for banning all affirmative action at the next opportunity. After all, the Roberts Court was not shy about taking the earliest chance to undermine *Brown*, a unanimous opinion celebrated as a zenith for the Court's civil rights accomplishments. The legal precedents for affirmative action are weaker, stretched between Justice Powell's plurality and Justice O'Connor's retired swing vote. Meanwhile, the political branches offer little solace, since even politicians who use affirmative action often dare not speak its name, and many now stress their support for preferences based on class, instead of race. Of course, class-based affirmative action, like financial-need scholarships, is a vital part of public policy advancing equal opportunity. But it cannot replace measures that directly address our history of legal, political and educational discrimination.

Ultimately, one part of the high public regard for bright, talented successful black leaders like Obama, Rice or Powell stems from public awareness that our country is still struggling to overcome racial barriers. Powell earned his success within a military and a Cabinet that proudly used affirmative action not simply as a benefit for individual "applicants" like him, not only as a "diversity" boost for his peers in military and government circles, but as an extrinsic value for the progress of our nation and the legitimacy of its leadership. As the first top-tier black presidential candidate, Obama has already advanced that progress another step. Yet win or lose, such examples remain too rare, as the first post–civil rights era cohort comes of age. Even Obama's potential election reveals this trend, for his elevation to the White House would leave the Senate without a single black member. We still need affirmative action in college, government and business—animated by race, class and equal opportunity—if we are ever going to reform America's resiliently segregated power structure.

11

Affirmative Action Is an Attack on American Identity

Roger Kimball

Roger Kimball is a conservative art critic, essayist, and social commentator.

The left-wing political and educational elites of the United States are determined to undermine traditional American values. By promoting affirmative action and its ideological ally, multiculturalism, these elites aim to create a 'value vacuum' that weakens a distinctive core of beliefs, attitudes, and commitments. While affirmative action pretends to promote equality, it enforces discrimination on the basis of sex and race. In the end, these left liberal elite doctrines are dangerous for they undermine the very keystone of American national identity.

What is your favorite bit of Orwellian Newspeak [referring to George Orwell's *1984*, about authoritarian government]? Near the top of my list is "affirmative action." It's such an emollient phrase, so redolent of cheeriness (savor the word "affirmative") and practicality ("action"). What it really means is "discrimination on the basis of sex, skin color, or some other item in the contemporary lexicon of victimology." But you can—almost—forget that while the pleasing phrase "affirmative action" echoes in your recollection.

I had occasion to ponder this anew last week when I attended a dinner in New York following the latest Intelligence

Squared [IQ2] debate. If you do not live in New York, you may not know about this splendid series of live debates organized by Robert Rosenkranz and the Rosenkranz Foundation. The resolution this evening was "It's time to end affirmative action." To me, the question is a no-brainer. *Of course* it is time to end "affirmative action." But that is not how some of my dinner partners saw it. Nor, as it happens, did the audience for the debate. Much to my surprise, they voted heartily against the resolution (44% against, 34% for, and 22% undecided). My surprise was only increased when I looked over the transcript of the debate (I had to miss the event itself): I thought those arguing for abolishing the practice of "affirmative action" had all the good arguments.

Alas, debates are not always won by the better arguments—a fact I know to my sorrow. When I participated in an Intelligence Squared debate last year on the motion "Hollywood has fueled anti-Americanism Abroad," I went to the debate thinking my side, which argued for the motion, would lose. But then we argued so much more persuasively than the other side (or so I thought) that I awaited the audience's vote with confident equanimity. It was a misplaced presumption, unfortunately, since we lost by a considerable margin. As I noted at the time, "in order to win an argument, you must appeal to the audience's emotions as well as their reason. What people yearn for, what they fear, is often more important than what they think in determining how they vote."

Notwithstanding the results of the IQ2 debate, it seems an opportune moment to step back and reflect on the phenomenon of "affirmative action" and its ideological comrade in arms, multiculturalism.

Anti-American Tribalism

A favorite weapon in the armory of multiculturalism is the lowly hyphen. When we speak of an African-American or Mexican-American or Asian-American these days, the aim is not descriptive but deconstructive. There is a polemical edge to it, a provocation. The hyphen does not mean "American, but hailing at some point in the past from someplace else." It means "only provisionally American: my allegiance is divided at best." (I believe something similar can be said about the feminist fad for hyphenating the bride's maiden name with her husband's surname. It is a gesture of independence that is also a declaration of divided loyalty.) It is curious to what extent the passion for hyphenation is fostered more by the liberal elite than the populations it is supposedly meant to serve. How does it serve them? Presumably by enhancing their sense of "self-esteem." Frederick Douglass saw through this charade some one hundred and fifty years ago. "No one idea," he wrote, "has given rise to more oppression and persecution toward colored people of this country than that which makes Africa, not America, their home."

The indispensable Ward Connerly would agree. Connerly has campaigned vigorously against affirmative action across the country. This of course has made him a pariah among the politically correct elite. It has also resulted in some humorous exchanges, such as this telephone interview with a reporter from the *New York Times* in 1997.

Reporter: What are you?

Connerly: I am an American.

Reporter: No, no, no! What *are* you?

Connerly: Yes, yes, yes! I am an American.

Reporter: That is not what I mean. I was told that you are African American. Are you ashamed to be African American?

Connerly: No, I am just proud to be an American.

Connerly went on to explain that his ancestry included Africans, French, Irish, and American Indians. It was too much for the poor reporter from our Paper of Record: "What does that make you?" he asked in uncomprehending exasperation. I suspect he was not edified by Connerly's cheerful response: "That makes me all-American."

The original effort to redress legitimate grievances— grievances embodied, for instance, in the discriminatory practices of Jim Crow—have mutated into new forms of discrimination.

The multicultural passion for hyphenation is not simply a fondness for syntactical novelty. It also bespeaks a commitment to the centrifugal force of anti-American tribalism. The division marked by the hyphen in African-American (say) denotes a political stand. It goes hand-in-hand with other items on the index of liberal desiderata [considered necessary or highly desirable]—the redistributive impulse behind efforts at "affirmative action," for example. Affirmative action was undertaken in the name of equality. But, as always seems to happen, it soon fell prey to the Orwellian logic from which the principle that "All animals are equal" gives birth to the transformative codicil [a supplement or appendix]: "but some animals are more equal than others."

Affirmative action is Orwellian in a linguistic sense, too, since what announces itself as an initiative to promote equality winds up enforcing discrimination precisely on the grounds that it was meant to overcome. Thus we are treated to the delicious, if alarming, contradiction of college applications that declare their commitment to evaluate candidates "without regard to race, gender, religion, ethnicity, or national origin" on page 1 and then helpfully inform you on page 2 that it is to your advantage to mention if you belong to any of the following designated victim groups. Among other things, a commitment to multiculturalism seems to dull one's sense of contradiction.

An Assault on American Identity

The whole history of affirmative action is instinct with that irony. The original effort to redress legitimate grievances— grievances embodied, for instance, in the discriminatory practices of Jim Crow—have mutated into new forms of discrimination. In 1940, Franklin Roosevelt established the Fair Employment Practices Committee because blacks were openly barred from war factory jobs. But what began as a Presidential Executive Order in 1961 directing government contractors to take "affirmative action" to assure that people be hired "without regard" for sex, race, creed, color, etc., has resulted in the creation of vast bureaucracies dedicated to discovering, hiring, and advancing people chiefly on the basis of those qualities. White is black, freedom is slavery, "without regard" comes to mean "with regard for nothing else.". . .

Multiculturalism and "affirmative action" are allies in the assault on the institution of American identity. As such, they oppose the traditional understanding of what it means to be an American—an understanding hinted at in 1782 by the French-born American farmer J. Hector St. John de Crève- coeur in his famous image of America as a country in which "individuals of all nations are melted into a new race of men." This crucible of American identity, this "melting pot," has two aspects. The negative aspect involves disassociating oneself from the cultural imperatives of one's country of origin. One sheds a previous identity before assuming a new one. One might preserve certain local habits and tastes, but they are essentially window-dressing. In essence one has left the past behind in order to become an American citizen.

The positive aspect of advancing the melting pot involves embracing the substance of American culture. The 1795 code for citizenship lays out some of the formal requirements.

> I do solemnly swear (1) to support the Constitution of the United States; (2) to renounce and abjure absolutely and entirely all allegiance and fidelity to any foreign prince, poten-

tate, state, or sovereignty of whom or which the applicant was before a subject or citizen; (3) to support and defend the Constitution and the laws of the United States against all enemies, foreign and domestic; (4) to bear true faith and allegiance to the same; and (5) (A) to bear arms on behalf of the United States when required by law, or (B) to perform noncombatant service in the Armed Forces of the United States when required by law . . .

For over two hundred years, this oath had been required of those wishing to become citizens. In 2003, Samuel Huntington tells us in his book *Who We Are*, federal bureaucrats launched a campaign to rewrite and weaken it. . . .

In America, there is a dangerous new tide of immigration from Asia, a variety of Muslim countries, and Latin America, especially from Mexico.

Americanization Was a Key Concern of Founding Fathers

It is often said that America is a nation of immigrants. In fact, as Huntington points out, America is a country that was initially a country of *settlers*. Settlers precede immigrants and make their immigration possible. The culture of those mostly English-speaking, predominantly Anglo-Protestant settlers defined American culture. Their efforts came to fruition with the generation of Franklin, Washington, Jefferson, Hamilton, and Madison.

The Founders are so denominated because they founded, they inaugurated a state. Immigrants were those who came later, who came from elsewhere, and who became American by embracing the Anglophone culture of the original settlers. The English language, the rule of law, respect for individual rights, the industriousness and piety that flowed from the Protestant work ethic—these were central elements in the culture disseminated by the Founders. And these were among the qualities embraced by immigrants when they became Americans. "Throughout American history," Huntington notes, "people who were not white Anglo-Saxon Protestants have become Americans by adopting America's Anglo-Protestant culture and political values. This benefitted them and the country."

[Supreme Court] Justice Louis Brandeis outlined the pattern in 1919. Americanization, he said, means that the immigrant "adopts the clothes, the manners, and the customs generally prevailing here . . . substitutes for his mother tongue the English language" and comes "into complete harmony with our ideals and aspirations and cooperate[s] with us for their attainment." Until the 1960s, the Brandeis model mostly prevailed. Protestant, Catholic, and Jewish groups, understanding that assimilation was the best ticket to stability and social and economic success, eagerly aided in the task of integrating their charges into American society.

New Immigrants Are Not Assiminating

The story is very different today. In America, there is a dangerous new tide of immigration from Asia, a variety of Muslim countries, and Latin America, especially from Mexico. The tide is new not only chronologically but also in substance. First, there is the sheer matter of numbers. More than 2,200,000 legal immigrants came to the U.S. from Mexico in the 1990s alone. The number of illegal Mexican immigrants is staggering. So is their birth rate. Altogether there are more than 8 million Mexicans in the U.S. Some parts of the Southwest are well on their way to becoming what [historian] Victor Davis Hanson calls "Mexifornia," "the strange society that is emerging as the result of a demographic and cultural revolution like no other in our times." A professor of Chicano Studies at the University of New Mexico gleefully predicts that by 2080 parts of the Southwest United States and Northern Mexico will join to form a new country, "La Republica del Norte."

The problem is not only one of numbers, though. Earlier immigrants made—and were helped and goaded by the ambient culture to make—concerted efforts to assimilate. Important pockets of these new immigrants are not assimilating, not learning English, not becoming or thinking of themselves primarily as Americans. The effect of these developments on American identity is disastrous and potentially irreversible.

The bottom line is that the traditional ideal of a distinctive American identity, forged out of many elements but unified around a core of beliefs, attitudes, and commitments is now up for grabs.

Anti-American Elites

Such developments are abetted by the left-wing political and educational elites of this country, whose dominant theme is the perfidy [violation] of traditional American values. Hence the passion for multiculturalism and the ideal of ethnic hyphenation that goes with it. This has done immense damage in schools and colleges as well as in the population at large. By removing the obligation to master English, multiculturalism condemns whole sub-populations to the status of permanent second-class citizens. By removing the obligation to adopt American values, it fosters what the German novelist Hermann Broch once called a "value vacuum," a sense of existential emptiness that breeds anomie [social instability] and the pathologies of nihilism [extreme skepticism].

As if in revenge for this injustice, however, multiculturalism also weakens the social bonds of the community at large. The price of imperfect assimilation is imperfect loyalty. Take the movement for bilingualism. Whatever it intended in theory, in practice it means *not* mastering English. It has notoriously left its supposed beneficiaries essentially monolingual, often semi-lingual. The only "bi" involved is a passion for bifurcation [division], which is fed by the accumulated resentments instilled by the anti-American multicultural ortho-doxy. Every time you call directory assistance or some large corporation and are told "Press One for English" and "*Para español oprime el numero dos*" it is another small setback for American identity.

Meanwhile, many prominent academics and even busi-nessmen come bearing the gospel of what John Fonte [Direc-tor of the Center for American Common Culture] has dubbed "transnational progressivism"—an anti-patriotic stew of po-litically correct ideas and attitudes distinguished partly by its penchant for vague but virtuous-sounding abstractions, partly by its moral smugness. It is a familiar litany. The philosopher Martha Nussbaum warns that "patriotic pride" is "morally dangerous" while University of Penn President Amy Gutmann reveals that she finds it "repugnant" for American students to learn that they are "above all, citizens of the United States" in-stead of partisans of her preferred abstraction, "democratic humanism." New York University's Richard Sennett denounces "the evil of a shared national identity" and concludes that the erosion of national sovereignty is "basically a positive thing." Cecilia O'Leary of American University identifies American patriotism as a right-wing, militaristic, male, white, Anglo, and repressive force, while Peter Spiro of Temple University says it "is increasingly difficult to use the word 'we' in the con-text of international affairs."

Of course, whenever the word "patriotism" comes up in left-wing circles, there is sure to be some allusion to Samuel Johnson's observation that "patriotism is the last refuge of scoundrels." Right on cue, George Lipsitz of the University of California sniffs that "in recent years refuge in patriotism has been the first resort of scoundrels of all sorts."

Naturally, Dr. Johnson's explanation to Boswell that he did not mean to disparage "a real and generous love of our coun-try" but only that "pretended patriotism" that is a "cloak for self-interest" is left out of account.

The bottom line is that the traditional ideal of a distinctive American identity, forged out of many elements but unified around a core of beliefs, attitudes, and commitments is now up for grabs. One academic epitomized the established attitude among our left-liberal elites when she expressed the hope that the United States would "never again be culturally 'united,' if united means 'unified' in beliefs and practices."

The Perils of Deconstruction

The combined effect of the multicultural enterprise has been to undermine the foundation of American national identity. Huntington speaks dramatically but not inaptly of "Deconstructing America.". . . "The deconstructionists," Huntington writes,

> promoted programs to enhance that status and influence of subnational racial, ethnic, and cultural groups. They encouraged immigrants to maintain their birth-country cultures, granted them legal privileges denied to native-born Americans, and denounced the idea of Americanization as un-American. They pushed the rewriting of history syllabi and textbooks so as to refer to the "peoples" of the United States in place of the single people of the Constitution. They urged supplementing or substituting for national history the history of subnational groups. They downgraded the centrality of English in American life and pushed bilingual education and linguistic diversity. They advocated legal recognition of group rights and racial preferences over the individual rights central to the American Creed. They justified their actions by theories of multiculturalism and the idea that diversity rather than unity or community should be America's overriding value. The combined effect of these efforts was to promote the deconstruction of the American identity that had been gradually created over three centuries.

Taken together, Huntington concludes, "these efforts by a nation's leaders to deconstruct the nation they governed were, quite possibly, without precedent in human history."

The various movements to deconstruct American identity and replace it with a multicultural "rainbow" or supra-national bureaucracy have made astonishing inroads in the last few decades and especially in the last several years. And, as Huntington reminds us, the attack on American identity has counterparts elsewhere in the West wherever the doctrine of multiculturalism has trumped the cause of national identity. The European Union—whose unelected leaders are as dedicated to multicultural shibboleths as they are to rule by top-down, anti-democratic bureaucracy—is a case in point. But the United States, the most powerful national state, is also the most attractive target for deconstruction.

It is a curious development that Huntington traces. In many respects, it corroborates James Burnham's observation, in *Suicide of the West* (1964), that "liberalism permits Western civilization to be reconciled to dissolution." For what we have witnessed with the triumph of multiculturalism is a kind of hypertrophy or perversion of liberalism, as its core doctrines are pursued to the point of caricature.

12

The Republican Party Shows Growing Support for Affirmative Action

Harry Stein

Harry Stein is a contributing editor of City Journal.

In 1981, Ronald Reagan, at his first presidential press conference, articulated the conservative case against affirmative action when he said the social policy had evolved into rigid quotas. A generation later, the GOP has drifted away from Reagan's principled position. In 2003, George W. Bush's administration, reversing a longstanding Republican Party position, defended affirmative action on the grounds of "diversity" in briefs filed to the United States Supreme Court. Unfortunately, this rationale was used by Justice Sandra Day O'Connor in Gratz v. Bollinger *to justify continuance of affirmative action. One reason why many white Republicans now support affirmative action is that they are terrified of being labeled "racists" by liberal demagogues.*

Ten years ago, the historic passage of California's Proposition 209 banning racial preferences in public contracting and university admissions seemed to promise that colorblind government would soon prevail nationwide. Today, though, affirmative action remains on the books almost everywhere in America. Those who've kept preferences alive include the usual coalition of left-wing activists, a strongly pro-affirmative-action media, business and civic groups anxious to avoid charges of racism, and, hardly least, judges who haven't hesitated to give their own political views the force of law. But what's arguably hurt the anti-preferences drive most has been the desertion of its formerly best ally: the Republican Party.

Nowhere has this Republican desertion been starker than in Michigan, where an almost exact replica of Prop. 209, mandating that the state "shall not discriminate against, or grant preferential treatment to, any individual or group on the basis of race, sex, color or ethnicity, or national origin" is on this fall's [2006] ballot. Led by its candidates for governor and U.S. Senator, the state GOP has emphatically distanced itself from the Michigan Civil Rights Initiative [MCRI].

Not only has GOP opposition enabled pro–affirmative-action forces to cast those fighting quotas as ideological pariahs, so far out of the mainstream (and, by implication, so tainted by racist bigotry) that not even *Republicans* want anything to do with them; it also has severely hampered the MCRI's fund-raising efforts, with many would-be contributors reluctant to cross the party leadership. "I can't tell you how many people have whispered in my ear, 'I'm with you, but I can't say anything publicly,'" confides a frustrated Jennifer Gratz, the MCRI's executive director and the former lead plaintiff in a landmark affirmative-action lawsuit against the University of Michigan. "There's just this fear of standing up and doing the right thing."

Even more disheartening, the Republican backtracking on preferences in Michigan reflects a quiet but steady shift in the national party, too, with the Bush administration undercutting affirmative-action foes—longtime GOP supporters—by embracing the "diversity" mantra that liberals so fervently preach.

Republicans Long Opposed Affirmative Action

The contrast with the GOP's principled recent past is striking. At his first press conference after assuming office in 1981,

President Ronald Reagan noted that many affirmative-action programs had become rigid quotas, adding: "I'm old enough to remember when quotas existed in the U.S. for the purpose of discrimination, and I don't want to see that happen again." Reagan's assistant attorney general for civil rights, the combative William Bradford Reynolds, echoed the anti-preferences view, judging affirmative action "demeaning because it says people are going to get ahead not because of what they can do but because of race." While federal bureaucrats and congressional Democrats often frustrated the Reagan administration's efforts to curb quotas, the president's position was never in doubt, and it set the tone for the party.

Black California businessman Ward Connerly was among the many drawn to the GOP by the force of Reagan's personality and straightforward commitment to principle, changing his party registration the very day after he met then-governor Reagan in 1969. Twenty-seven years later, after discovering as a trustee of the University of California system the extent to which skin color determined admission to top campuses like UCLA and Berkeley, he was leading the fight for Prop. 209. Then, as now, the viciousness of the opposition (headed by future [John] Kerry campaign guru Bob Shrum) knew no bounds. Television ads attacking the measure depicted cross burnings and police dogs, seeking to link anti-preferences forces with the ugliest anti-integration backlash of the civil rights era; Prop. 209 foes at Cal State Northridge actually invited KKK leader David Duke to campus to speak on *behalf* of the measure.

But support for Prop. 209 was broad and deep, and included many influential figures in business and politics. Most notably, its chief sponsor, Republican governor Pete Wilson, effectively countered the other side's race-baiting by arguing that those fighting to make race a nonfactor in government decision making were abiding by the civil rights crusade's true values. "It is time for those who have resisted Prop. 209 to acknowledge that equal rights under law, not special preferences, is the law of the land," he declared. "A measure that eliminates any form of discrimination based on race and gender violates no one's constitutional rights."

In the end, 209 passed comfortably, with 54 percent of the vote. Republican Party support was "vital," recalls Connerly. "They provided us with a lot of foot soldiers and, even more essential, a critical mass of support—because nobody ever likes to be left standing alone, especially when it comes to race."

The mere hint of a "racism charge" transforms even normally principled leaders into panderers and cowards.

The same scenario played out in Washington State in 1998, where Connerly led the fight for that state's anti-preferences measure, I-200. While some Republican moderates, including former governor Dan Evans, opposed the initiative, the conservative-controlled state GOP enthusiastically endorsed it; and though foes outspent supporters by nearly three to one— with such liberal-leaning corporate Goliaths as Eddie Bauer, Microsoft, and Starbucks contributing heavily to the "No on 200" campaign—the initiative passed by a whopping 58 to 42 percent. The margin is even more impressive when examined in its particulars. According to exit polls, 80 percent of Republicans supported I-200, but so did 62 percent of independents and 41 percent of Democrats. In fact, Democratic senator Patty Murray was one of the measure's most vocal critics, and 43 percent of her supporters voted for it.

There's little evidence of any change in public attitudes about racial preferences since. The Republican rank and file remains especially united: a poll of Michigan GOP voters earlier this year, for instance, showed 78 percent backing the MCRI. So the party's turnabout on the issue can seem bewildering.

Republicans Shift Political Tactics

The shift on preferences clearly involves naked political calculation. With a mere 8 percent of blacks voting GOP in 2004, party leaders have made no secret of their eagerness to try to splinter the most reliable of Democratic voting blocs. Over the last year and a half, party chairman Ken Mehlman has appeared before numerous black audiences, preaching the virtues of Republicanism. As the *New York Times* noted in a lengthy and laudatory piece on Mehlman in July, the GOP chairman believes that "Republican advocacy of economic policies that would give more power to individuals rather than to government—like health saving accounts—would appeal to middle-class black voters as much as it would to whites."

All well and good. But as the *Times* (approvingly) points out, Mehlman's outreach agenda hardly ends there. He has also repeatedly "apologized for what he described as the racially polarized politics of some Republicans over the past 25 years" and for "what civil rights leaders view as decades of racial politics practiced or countenanced by Republicans. One example they point to is the first President Bush's use of the escape of Willie Horton, a black convicted murderer, to portray his Democratic opponent in the 1988 election, Michael S. Dukakis, as soft on crime."

That Republicans have long cynically exploited race is a given for the *Times's* "civil rights leaders" and liberals in general. But that the Republican chairman now accepts such a proposition is astonishing. In fact, it's easy to make the case that, in recent years, the civil rights establishment and its Democratic allies have been the true cynics—and effective ones—in playing the race card to achieve electoral and policy ends. One can argue that the Horton ad, tough as it was, made a legitimate point, highlighting a significant Dukakis policy failure. But no such claim would be possible about the ad that the NAACP produced in 2000, linking George W.

Bush to the brutal murder of a black man, James Byrd, by racist thugs. Consider, too, the shameless smear campaign that Senate liberals (with a substantial assist from the mainstream media) waged against Judge Charles Pickering, a man who admirably stood up for civil rights in Mississippi at a time when few whites did so, yet who now found himself portrayed as soft on cross burners and thus unfit for a seat on the Fifth Circuit Court.

Republicans Afraid to Be Called Racists

But another reality has also prompted the Republican shift on race: race remains the most volatile and, for white politicians, the most terrifying issue in American life. The mere hint of a "racism" charge transforms even normally principled leaders into panderers and cowards.

What affirmative action says is that blacks are fundamentally deficient and in need of special compensation based on events none of us even lived through.

The brilliant social critic Shelby Steele gives the best explanation for this fear. Of mixed race himself, Steele writes of the paramount role that "white guilt" plays in contemporary American race relations. Conscious of the stain of the nation's discriminatory past, whites often feel a powerful need "to demonstrate to the world that they're not bigots." They do so most readily by deferring, at least publicly, to the civil rights establishment on matters of racial justice.

Ward Connerly has repeatedly witnessed this dynamic at work firsthand. "I've often had the experience of speaking in a room of 100 people, and knowing that 99 of them agree with me," he says. "But if there's one angry black person in the audience who disagrees, that person controls the room. He'll go on about the last 400 years, and institutional racism, and 'driving while black,' and the other 99 will just sit there and fold like a cheap accordion."

As official Republican support has fallen away, it is largely black conservatives like Connerly and Steele who have continued to lead the challenge to government-sanctioned discrimination. Unburdened by white guilt, keenly attuned to the damage that the preferences regime has done not only to society at large but to its purported beneficiaries, they do not hesitate to speak uncomfortable truths that conventional politicians shun. They passionately argue that racial preferences, by their very nature, convey the message that—unlike other Americans—blacks can't succeed by merit; that even as they encourage blacks to wrap themselves in the mantle of victimhood, preferences stigmatize all black achievement as illegitimate. Worse still, the racial spoils system has done nothing to help those whose lives are in the most desperate disarray: the black urban underclass.

"What affirmative action says is that blacks are fundamentally deficient and in need of special compensation based on events none of us even lived through," asserts columnist and radio talk-show host Mychal Massie. "I frankly have to wonder whether those who continue to countenance racial preferences truly even care about the problems plaguing black America, because they obviously don't care whether it works. It does nothing, *nothing*, to address out-of-wedlock births, fatherlessness, the illiteracy rate, attitudes about education, any of the issues that are destroying the black community in the country. It only allows those who support it to feel virtuous while they *avoid* facing those issues."

Adds Massie: "It is frankly inconceivable to me that anyone who claims to believe in fairness would countenance that people in Michigan are being denied a seat in the classroom based on nothing more than the fact that they're white. That is just as vile as it was when Bull Connor and Orval Faubus locked people out because they were black."

Bush Administration Abandons Friends

It was an old-fashioned liberal, a veteran philosophy professor at the University of Michigan named Carl Cohen, who set in motion the events that eventually led to the Michigan Civil Rights Initiative. A former head of the state ACLU and a vigorous defender of individual rights, Cohen filed a Freedom of Information request in 1996 that forced the university to lay bare its admissions procedures. The evidence showed not only that university officials "had discriminated by race but that they intended to do so, they made no bones about it," Cohen says. Indeed, the documents revealed that the admissions office had two distinct tracks: one for whites and the other for protected minorities.

For preference foes, the Supreme Court battle was a disappointment in another crucial respect: it signaled the Bush administration's abandonment of the cause.

Within months of the revelation, both the undergraduate division of the university and the law school faced legal challenges. The 17-year-old daughter of a police sergeant in a working-class Detroit suburb and the first in her family aiming for college, Jennifer Gratz had been turned down by the Ann Arbor campus that she'd long dreamed of attending in favor of "some friends of mine, kids I sat next to in class," who clearly didn't measure up to her academically. "I really had trouble at first believing they would do that," she says now, laughing at her naivety. "It was so against everything I'd been taught was right—that you treat everyone fairly and equally." In short order, she signed on as a plaintiff.

By the time the Supreme Court handed down its twin decisions in *Gratz v. Bollinger* and *Grutter v. Bollinger* in 2003, Gratz had long since graduated from college—at the University of Michigan's less prestigious Dearborn campus. By allowing the university in effect to continue to use race as a factor in admissions—and a recent study from the Center for Equal Opportunity found the school's discrimination against white and Asian applicants to be worse than ever—those rulings sparked the next phase of the battle against preferences: the push to institute a state constitutional ban, via the MCRI.

For preference foes, the Supreme Court battle was a disappointment in another crucial respect: it signaled the Bush administration's abandonment of the cause. True, the administration, acting ostensibly on behalf of Gratz and the others unfairly denied admission to the university, submitted two *amicus curiae* briefs to the court, arguing that the University of Michigan's quota-based admissions system was "plainly unconstitutional." But the briefs also provided key fodder for the other side by agreeing that "diversity," that vague feel-good catchall that liberals have enshrined as a primary good, "is an important and entirely legitimate government objective."

As journalist Christopher Caldwell noted at the time, "The Bush memos are the most important substantive defense of affirmative action ever issued by a sitting president. If the Court accepts the president's reasoning, it will have rescued affirmative action from what appeared to be a terminal constitutional illogic. More than that—it will have secured for this rickety program an indefinite constitutional legitimacy." Caldwell proved prescient, the administration's "diversity" argument being precisely the one that Justice Sandra Day O'Connor cited for her pivotal vote in the 5-4 decision. "Effective participation by members of all racial and ethnic groups in the civil life of our nation is essential if the dream of one nation, indivisible, is to be realized," O'Connor declared, writing for the majority.

Opinion divides on the anti-preferences side about who bears the greatest responsibility for the administration's revised affirmative-action stance. According to Terrence Pell, lead attorney for the Center for Individual Rights, which represented the plaintiffs in the U-M cases, "We'd been assured the Justice Department was going to take a strong position that diversity was not a compelling interest and that [then–solicitor general] Ted Olson's shop had already written a brief taking on the diversity rationale. But this started a huge fight and [White House counsel] Alberto Gonzales put his foot down and forced the change in direction."

A pandering Republican approach is just as likely to put off many voters, including blacks who might otherwise find the party's economic and social policies attractive.

Ward Connerly, who has again helped lead the fight against preferences in Michigan, speculates that the administration's skittishness on the issue goes even higher. He recalls that when he first encountered then-governor George W. Bush in Texas, the future president was "extremely open" on the issue of preferences. "He threw his arm around me and said, 'I want you to come up to the mansion, we've got to get together and talk about this.' And I thought, 'Wow, this is great,'" Connerly recalls. But when he tried to follow up, Connerly recounts, "I was told that Karl Rove doesn't think that's a good idea right now, we'll get back to you later. To this day, it's never happened."

Republican Pondering Backfires

For the first five years of his presidency, Bush refused to appear before the NAACP's annual convention, citing, as he did in 2004, "the rhetoric and the names they've called me." That vituperation has continued unabated—perhaps even escalated. "Their idea of equal rights," NAACP chairman Julian Bond said of Republicans this past February [2006], "is the American flag and the Confederate swastika flying side by side." Nonetheless, the president has now made his peace with the organization. In a platitude-heavy address to its 2006 convention, he spoke of how "racism still lingers in America" and referred warmly to Jesse Jackson and Julian Bond. "I understand that many African-Americans distrust my political party," he added. "I want to change the relationship."

There's no indication, though, that a changed relationship will happen anytime soon. As Illinois senator Barack Obama, a Harvard Law School pal of GOP chairman Mehlman, told the *New York Times*, "The agenda of the Republican Party keeps getting in the way of that outreach." Or, to put it more bluntly, it is impossible to out-pander the Democrats.

In fact, a pandering Republican approach is just as likely to put off many voters, including blacks who might otherwise find the party's economic and social policies attractive. Says Connerly, "Deep down, black people deeply resent being treated like children. Ultimately, the way to appeal to blacks is the same way you do to whites, by showing you believe in things and fighting for them."

What the party's revised stance on race has done—aside from bolstering a civil rights establishment whose prestige had sharply declined and that remains unremittingly hostile to all that the Republican Party stands for—is leave longtime allies more vulnerable than ever to the toxic charge of "racism.". . .

A year ago, polls showed the MCRI winning easily with upward of 60 percent. Now the numbers have tightened, with one of the most recent polls showing it in a dead heat, and the other showing it ahead by four points.

But whatever the result—and voters notoriously lie to pollsters on issues involving race—the party's role in the contest is something many thoughtful Republicans will regard with sorrow. If the MCRI loses, it will demonstrate yet again the damage done by the party's flight from principle; if it wins, it will stand as even more evidence that the GOP is on the wrong side not only of its base, but of history.

"It truly makes you yearn for a return of leaders like Ronald Reagan or Pete Wilson," says Connerly of recent events in Michigan. "People who knew what they believed and weren't afraid to act on their beliefs. You really have to wonder where people like that have gone."

Organizations to Contact

The editors have compiled the following list of organizations concerned with the issues debated in this book. The descriptions are derived from materials provided by the organizations. All have publications or information available for interested readers. The list was compiled on the date of publication of the present volume; the information provided here may change. Be aware that many organizations take several weeks or longer to respond to inquiries, so allow as much time as possible.

American Association for Affirmative Action (AAAA)
888 16th Street, NW, Suite 800, Washington, DC   20006
(202) 349-9855 • fax: (202) 355-1399
e-mail: ExecAdminAsst@affirmativeaction.org
Web site: www.affirmativeaction.org

Founded in 1974, the American Association for Affirmative Action (AAAA) is a nonprofit association of public and private sector professionals dedicated to eradicating all forms of invidious discrimination. AAAA provides training and educational programs to promote professional growth and development of its 2,000 individual and corporate members. The Web site provides information on many higher education scholarships, professional development, and training.

American Civil Liberties Union (ACLU)
125 Broad Street, 18th Floor, New York, NY   10004
(212) 607-3300 • fax: (212) 607-3318
Web site: www.aclu.org/racialjustice/aa

The American Civil Liberties Union (ACLU) Racial Justice Program seeks to fight racism by protecting and advancing the constitutional rights of minorities in education, employment, state contracting, and numerous other areas. The advocacy program promotes affirmative action though litigation, community organizing and training, legislative initiatives, and public education. The nonprofit organization's Web site offers a wide array of publications, legal documents, legislative documents, resources, fact sheets, and information on court cases. It also provides links to local affiliates.

American Civil Rights Institute (ACRI)

P.O. Box 188350, Sacramento, CA   95818
(916) 444-2278 • fax: (916) 444-2279
e-mail: feedback@acri.org
Web site: www.acri.org

The American Civil Rights Institute (ACRI) is a nonprofit civil rights organization created to educate the general public on the effects of racial and gender preferences. The institute believes that civil rights are individual rights and that government policies should not advocate group rights over individual ones. Established by Ward Connerly, the institute has successfully led the effort to ban racial preferences by supporting California Proposition 209, Washington's I-200, One Florida, and Michigan's Proposal 2. The organization continues to monitor the implementation of these statewide ballot initiatives. The ACRI publishes the *Egalitarian Newsletter,* and its Web site links to news articles and like-minded organizations' Web sites.

By Any Means Necessary (BAMN)

P.O. Box 24834, Detroit, MI   48224
(313) 438-3748
e-mail: letters@bamn.com
Web site: www.bamn.com

The Coalition to Defend Affirmative Action, Integration, Immigrant Rights, and Fight for Equality By Any Means Necessary (BAMN) is a national organization dedicated to building a new mass civil rights movement to defend the gains of the 1960s civil rights movement and to advance the struggle for equality in American society. The organization rejects all claims that the inequalities of race and gender and the oppression of racism and sexism can be adequately explained as natural or inevitable consequences of human nature, original sin, biological destiny, or the supposed deficiencies of various ethnic cultures. The Web site offers fact sheets, press releases, position statements, and online petitions.

Center for Advancement of Racial and Ethnic Equity (CAREE)
American Council on Education, Washington, DC   20036
(202) 939-9300
e-mail: comments@ace.nche.edu
Web site: www.acenet.edu

Formerly the Office of Minorities in Higher Education, the American Center on Education's Center for Advancement of Racial and Ethnic Equity (CAREE) speaks out about the importance of diversity and inclusion at all levels of higher education. Its core mission is to monitor and report on the progress of blacks, Hispanics, Asian Americans, and American Indians in postsecondary education and to improve their educational and employment opportunities in higher education. The center offers a variety of diversity-related initiatives and programs, along with annual status reports on minorities in higher education.

Center for Economic Opportunity (CEO)
7700 Leesburg Pike, Suite 231, Falls Church, VA   22043
(703) 442-0066 • fax: (703) 442-0449
e-mail: lchavez@ceousa.org
Web site: www.ceousa.org

The Center for Economic Opportunity (CEO) is the nation's only conservative think tank devoted to issues of race and ethnicity. It believes that national policies should not further divide an already multiethnic and multiracial nation. Instead, the center aims to unify the nation by advocating colorblind public policies and seeking to block expansion of racial preferences and to prevent their use in employment, education, and voting. The center offers a Web-based antidiscrimination hotline where, on the behalf of the complainant, the organization may contact the alleged discriminator and may help the complainant find a lawyer.

Center for Individual Rights (CIR)

1233 20th Street, NW, Suite 300, Washington, DC   20036
(202) 833-8400 • fax: (202) 833-8410
Web site: www.cir-usa.org

The Center for Individual Rights (CIR) is a nonprofit public interest law firm dedicated to the defense of individual liberties against the authority of federal and state governments. It aggressively litigates and publicizes a handful of carefully selected cases that challenge excessive government regulation, unconstitutional state action, and other modern state entanglements. In 1997, the CIR filed the landmark lawsuit against the University of Michigan (*Grutter v. Bollinger*) challenging its use of racial preferences. The Web site offers press releases and court decisions dealing with civil rights, freedom of speech, first amendment, equal protection, and congressional authority.

Diversity Web

Association of American Colleges and Universities
Washington, DC   20009
e-mail: diversityweb@aacu.org
Web site: www.diversityweb.org

Diversity Web is a project of the Association of American Colleges and Universities' Office of Diversity, Equity, and Global Initiatives. Its central belief is that diversity and global knowledge are essential elements of any effort to foster civic engagement among today's college students. The project helps colleges and universities establish diversity as a comprehensive institutional commitment and educational priority. The project publishes the quarterly journal *Diversity and Democracy*.

National Association for the Advancement of Colored People (NAACP)

4805 Mt. Hope Drive, Baltimore, MD 21215
(877) NAACP-98 (toll-free) • fax: (410) 358-1607
e-mail: washingtonbureau@naacpnet.org
Web site: www.naacp.org

Since its founding in 1909, the NAACP strives to ensure the political, educational, social, and economic equality rights of all people and to eliminate racial hatred and racial discrimination. The organization supports affirmative action policies and practices by states to ensure equal opportunities for minorities and women. The organization believes that affirmative action does not give unfair advantage to minorities and women at the workplace or in the college admission process. Instead, it protects qualified applicants and workers from institutional racism. The organization publishes *Crisis* magazine.

National Organization for Women

1100 H Street NW, 3rd Floor, Washington, DC 20005
(202) 628-8669 • Fax: (202) 785-8576
Web site: www.now.org

The National Organization for Women (NOW) is the largest organization of feminist activists in America. It has 500,000 contributing members and 550 chapters in all fifty states and the District of Columbia. Since 1966, NOW has asserted that women of color suffer from the double burden of race and sex discrimination. The organization is committed to fighting for equal opportunities in all areas including employment, education, and reproductive rights. The organization issues action alerts, legislative updates, and provides news, plus news archives, relating to affirmative action.

Office of Federal Contract Compliance Programs

United States Department of Labor, Washington, DC 20210
(886) 4-USA-DOL
Web site: www.dol.gov/esa/ofccp

The Office of Federal Contract Compliance Programs is responsible for ensuring that contractors and subcontractors doing business with the federal government take affirmative action and do not discriminate, ensuring that all individuals have an equal opportunity for employment without regard to race, color, religion, sex, national origin, disability, or status as a Vietnam-era or special disabled veteran. The Web site provides links to all relevant laws, small business guides, employment resource directories, and numerous guidance documents.

Bibliography

Books

Terry H. Anderson	*The Pursuit of Fairness: A History of Affirmative Action.* New York: Oxford University Press, 2004.
Derrick A. Bell	*Silent Covenants: Brown v. Board of Education and the Unfulfilled Hopes for Racial Reform.* New York: Oxford University Press, 2006.
Benjamin Bowser	*The Black Middle Class: Social Mobility—and Vulnerability.* Boulder, CO: Lynee Rienner, 2007.
Faye J. Crosby	*Affirmative Action Is Dead: Long Live Affirmative Action.* New Haven, CT: Yale University Press, 2004.
Thomas J. Davis	*Race Relations in America: A Reference Guide with Primary Documents.* Westport, CT: Greenwood Press, 2006.
Michael Dyson	*Debating Race with Michael Dyson.* New York: Basic Civitas Books, 2007.
Patricia Gurin	*Defending Diversity: Affirmative Action at the University of Michigan.* Ann Arbor: University of Michigan Press, 2004.

Steve Holbert and   *The Color of Guilt and Innocence:*
Lisa Rose   *Racial Profiling and Police Practices in*
                    America. San Ramon, CA: Page
                    Marque Press, 2004.

Ira Katznelson   *When Affirmative Action Was White:*
                    An Untold History of Racial Inequality
                    in Twentieth-Century America. New
                    York: Norton, 2005.

Bob Laird   *The Case for Affirmative Action in*
                    University Admissions. Berkeley, CA:
                    Bay Tree, 2005.

Kevin Lang   *Poverty and Discrimination.*
                    Princeton, NJ: Princeton University
                    Press, 2007.

John H.   *Winning the Race: Beyond the Crisis*
McWhorter   *in Black America.* New York: Gotham
                    Books, 2005.

Jamillah Moore   *Race and College Admissions: A Case*
                    for Affirmative Action. Jefferson, NC:
                    McFarland, 2005.

Michalle E.   *Managing Diversity: Toward a*
Mor-Barak   *Globally Inclusive Workplace.*
                    Thousand Oaks, CA: Sage, 2005.

Barbara Perry   *The Michigan Affirmative Action*
                    Cases. Lawrence: University of Kansas
                    Press, 2007.

Peter Sacks   *Tearing Down the Gates: Confronting*
                    the Class Divide in American
                    Education. Berkeley: University of
                    California Press, 2007.

Mark Ivor Satin   *Racial Middle: The Politics We Need Now.* Boulder, CO: Westview Press, 2004.

Peter Schmidt   *Color and Money: How Rich White Kids Are Winning the War Over College Affirmative Action.* New York: Palgrave Macmillan, 2007.

Thomas Sowell   *Affirmative Action Around the World: An Empirical Study.* New Haven, CT: Yale University Press, 2004.

Greg Stohr   *A Black and White Case: How Affirmative Action Survived Its Greatest Legal Challenge.* Princeton, NJ: Bloomberg Press, 2004.

Tim J. Wise   *Affirmative Action: Racial Preference in Black and White.* New York: Routledge, 2005.

Robert Zelnick   *Swing Dance: Justice O'Connor and the Michigan Muddle.* Stanford, CA: Hoover Institution Press, Stanford University, 2004.

Periodicals

Peter Beinart   "The Trailblazers," *Time*, May 26, 2008.

Derrick Bell   "Desegregation's Demise," *The Education Digest*, December 2007.

Dorothy A. Brown   "Taking *Grutter* Seriously: Getting Beyond the Numbers," *Houston Law Review* 43, no. 1, 2006.

Ronald Brownstein	"How the South Rose Again," *American Prospect*, February 2006.
Ellis Cose	"Should Black People Let Affirmative Action Die? No," *Ebony*, January 2008.
Gary Gerstle	"Affirmative Action: The Last Stand," *Dissent*, Spring 2006.
Madison J. Gray	"Nationwide Attack on Affirmative Action," *Black Enterprise*, February 2007.
Susan W. Kaufmann	"The History and Impact of State Initiatives to Eliminate Affirmative Action," *New Directions for Teaching and Learning*, no. 111, Fall 2007.
Samantha Levine	"Taking Action to Admit," *U.S. News & World Report*, June 4, 2007.
Maurice Mangum	"Testing Competing Explanations of Black Opinions on Affirmative Action," *The Policy Studies Journal* 36, no. 3, 2008.
Amanda Marcotte	"Multiculture Club," *American Prospect*, May 2008.
Hildy Medina	"The Current State of Diversity in the Workplace," *Hispanic Business*, April 2008.
Ruben Navarrette, Jr.	"Race to the Top," *Hispanic*, March 2007.

Peter Schmidt — "'Bakke' Set a New Path to Diversity for Colleges," *The Chronicle of Higher Education*, June 20, 2008.

Thomas Sowell — "Let the Asian Students Succeed," *Hoover Digest*, Winter 2007.

Armstrong Williams — "Should Black People Let Affirmative Action Die? Yes." *Ebony*, January 2008.

Index

A

AAAA (American Association for Affirmative Action), 109
ABC/ESPN, 49
ACLU (American Civil Liberties Union), 104, 109–110
Acosta, Andrea, 37
ACRI (American Civil Rights Institute), 8, 110
Admissions
    gender and, 53, 54, 64–67
    "holistic" approach to, 20–21
    "plus factors" in, 33, 34
    point system in, 34–35
    Supreme Court and, 22
Advocacy, in media, 36–37
African-Americans, 87–88, 89, 103
Alito, Samuel, 84–85
American Association for Affirmative Action (AAAA), 109
American citizenship, 90–91, 94
American Civil Liberties Union (ACLU), 104, 109–110
American Civil Rights Institute, 8
American Civil Rights Institute (ACRI), 8, 110
American Council of Education, 70
American Educational Research Association, 40–41
American Enterprise Institute for Public Policy Research, 66
American identity
    affirmative action and, 86–89
    immigrants and, 93
    multiculturalism and, 87–90, 93, 95, 96
    undermining of, 94–95
American University, 94
Americanization, 90–92, 95
Amherst (MA), 66
Anglo-Protestant culture/values, 91–92
Anomie (social instability), 93
Anti-Americanism, 87–89, 93–96
Asia, 92
Asian-Americans, 87–88
Assimilation, 92–93
Athens (GA), 63
Attention Deficit Disorder, 58
Augusta Chronicle (newspaper), 24, 25, 29

B

Bacon, Jacqueline, 22
Baird, Vanessa, 39
Bakke, Regents of the University of California v., 16–17, 33, 41
Balance/objectivity, in reporting, 31–32, 35–39
Balkin, Jack, 81
Ballot initiatives, affirmative action
    California Proposition 209, 8, 17, 19, 20, 33–34, 78, 97–100
    Michigan Civil Rights Initiative, 8, 98, 100, 104, 107–108
    Washington State Initiative 200, 8, 17, 34, 78, 100
BAMN (By Any Means Necessary), 110–111
Bangor (ME), 60